THE MEANING IN THE MAKING

The why and how
behind our human
need to create

SEAN TUCKER

At the end of select chapters throughout this book, you will see a QR code at the bottom of the page. It will look something like this:

It will take you to a web page showing you some of the images and videos mentioned in the chapter.

To use it, simply open your mobile phone camera and point it at the QR code, hold it for a few seconds, and then follow the prompt to open the web page on your mobile device. Some older phones may require that you download a dedicated "QR code reader" app.

Order

It's blue hour, and the final glow of the day is fading fast.

I'm lying with my skinny nine-year-old frame on the flat of my back in a wide, sandy riverbed staring up at the inky purple sky as stars fast flare into view. The sand still holds the warmth of the day while a cool breeze begins to blow overhead. There is an earthy, spicy smell in the air and the sound of crickets ring all around.

In this remote corner of Africa, in the middle of the Botswanan bushveld, there are no city lights to steal from the stars so they begin to blaze against the black of night.

First, the brighter stars, then smaller ones hove into view, and soon countless pinpricks of light of various intensities and colours make themselves known.

Directly over my head, I can see the Milky Way smeared across the heavens, a great band of light, and as my eyes adjust it separates into a million tiny luminescent pinpricks, the dark trees overhanging the river like an organic black frame of spidery shadows.

I would usually give a casual upward glance at the night sky, and with unseeing familiarity consider it, as most of humankind always has, like a great sheet spread above.

A firmament.

However, not this night.

Days before, in school, we had been shown a picture of our galaxy as a spinning disc made up of a multitude of stars in infinite space, our little planet positioned on one of its spiralling arms. Our teacher told us that that is what we see when we look up into the night sky and see the Milky Way, that we are in fact looking from our position on one of its limbs into the rotating centre of its colossal disc.

Lying there, looking up, I suddenly recall that fact, and what was a peaceful minute of childlike contemplation turns into a moment of absolute terror.

I feel like I'm falling, tumbling into the infinite.

I'm no longer lying on the still-warm sand of a dry river bed, looking up at the firmament of the night sky; now I'm lying pinned to a spinning ball of rock, looking down, not up, into the plane of our galaxy, with its billion suns, as it whirls its way at breakneck speed through unending space, and I feel as if whatever force holds me in place may let go at any second, and if it does, I will be released to fall into endless nothingness.

It scares the hell out of me, but I stay with it.

It's also utterly exhilarating.

My heart is pounding in my chest at the enormity of the thought—of the fact.

There is a pull to that same nothingness as well, a beckoning.

It takes considerable courage, but I slowly stretch out my arms and legs, forming a star shape on the ground, in an act of letting go, of releasing myself to fall.

What gave me the courage to stretch out my arms in the face of that gaping void was Order:

The Order which holds the Chaos at bay.

This moment I've described is burned into my memory because it was the first time I can remember feeling those two things in such a palpable fashion: the Chaos and the Order.

The Chaos of the abyss in front of me and the Order that held me firm to this rock, as it has every day before and since.

At that moment, I realised how powerful that Order is—the proof being that it could give a nine-year-old such courage in the face of such a big truth. I had faith in that Order and believed it would hold me in place even as I stared it in the face.

But it was also the moment I stopped naively trusting in the permanence of that Order. I questioned it for the first time. I played with the idea that our planet could slow its spin and that gravity could fail. I imagined that day, millions of years hence, when the sun would expand to swallow us up (another "fun" fact our teacher had gifted a class of nine-year-olds that week). It was a moment when I realised it could all fail, and Chaos could take over.

Things could change. Things will change.

♂

It's not really important for our purposes here, what you attribute that Order to. Whether it's some "higher power" with religious structures built around it or just the immutable laws of nature. Either way, in our most awake and aware moments, we are in equal measure wonderstruck and terrified by the way things seem to just work, without our assistance, and often without our understanding. Ironically, I think it's this fascination that first drives both priests and scientists into their respective careers.

But even as we attempt to examine and explain the Order, whether analytically or spiritually, we also know Chaos is out there, and we know deep down it will ultimately win.

If you come from a religious tradition, you likely subscribe to some kind of vision of Armageddon, or Apocalypse, or Ragnarok. It's the historical mystics, who predated the scientific method, reminding us through countless stories told to millions of listeners in hundreds of cultures, that this Order won't last. Things will ultimately move toward Chaos.

If you're a scientist, you believe in Entropy. The second law of thermodynamics tells us that, left to its own devices, the universe and all things will move into greater states of dis-Order over time.

But that's the point; we human beings don't leave anything to their own devices. We control, we influence, we change, we bend and even break, and at our very best, we create.

And that's what we're here to talk about.

Fashioning and forming.

Moulding and forging.

Making.

Creating.

&

Let's start by trying to answer the question, "Why are human beings such creative creatures?" Why are we compelled to make?

My humbly offered answer to that impossibly large question is that we make because we are constantly trying to pull Order from Chaos.

I think we collectively intuited, long before science gave us the language, which way the universe is bending, and every act of creation on our part is in defiance of Entropy. Every time we pick up a paintbrush and choose complementary hues to apply to the canvas, or arrange elements through our camera viewfinders to create a pleasing composition, or press fingers into wet clay to wrestle form from a shapeless lump, we are bending things back toward Order and wrestling them from Chaos.

Even as I sit here now furiously typing away on this keyboard, every "click" and every "clack" feels like a tiny battle won, bending the universe imperceptibly away from disorder and toward life.

I don't know about you, but the days I make something are the days that leave me feeling the most fulfilled and that lead to nights of the most peaceful sleep.

We are driven to create because it comforts us in the face of impending disorder. We know that no matter how much we make, we cannot ultimately turn the tide, but we can make things to help us make sense of life. We can make things to ward off the darkness.

It's why cavemen painted their walls with scenes from their daily lives, and in the case of the works discovered at Lascaux dating back some 20,000 years, even used the very contours of the rock to render their images three-dimensional. They daubed depictions of animals, humans, and even abstract symbols onto the walls in beautiful detail, perhaps to feel more in control of the chaotic forces that dictated the direction of their lives.

It's why ancient Mesopotamians carved the *Epic of Gilgamesh* into tablets 4,000 years ago. They created stories to address the great questions, and attempt to describe the things they didn't understand. Why are we here? Why is life so full of pain and hardship? What do we do with the time we are given? What are our limits? How do we face our own mortality?

It's why Bronze Age humans erected stone circles 5,000 years ago. Experts are still arguing about the exact reasons they spent huge amounts of time and energy to cut colossal stones, hauling them across the landscape in order to upend them in circles. All we have are theories, but I think it's safe to say from the way these structures are often aligned astronomically, that this was some form of tangible expression of the way they saw the universe and their place in it. Perhaps more than that, it made them feel more in control of the reality they found themselves in.

Of course, these structures could have also had religious significance, but even then, what is worship, ritual, and sacrifice if not an attempt to first personalize those forces that bring rains to crops, or an end to sickness, and then bargain with them to work in our favour?

To bargain with Chaos and bring Order.

These historical acts of making weren't just about interior decorating, or architecture, or having something to read in the bathroom. Creating helped these peoples deal with and describe a world in which they felt that heady mix of competent and completely powerless, and in that regard, precious little has changed. We are still making things to communicate what we intuit to others, to pull answers from questions, and Order from Chaos.

But this is where art differs from science and religion because, in their own ways, each of the latter seeks to formulate Order in certain terms.

Science is trying to wrestle Order from Chaos through rigorous examination and testing, looking for patterns and attempting to explain them through the prism of the rules we have established to date.

But what about everything we can't explain scientifically?

Well, for many, this is where religion steps in and seeks to explain the mysteries we haven't formalised in scientific laws. Similarly, each religious branch tries to answer all the great "why" questions through their own particular lenses, and then most attempt to codify Order into our lives by giving us the "rules for living in an orderly fashion."

However, science is a long way off in answering all the questions we have, and for most, religion is too prescriptive and limiting. So what do we do with our human experience? How do we share what we intuit about "life, the universe, and everything" when we don't have scientific proofs or religious doctrine to support what we believe we've seen, felt, or experienced?

We make.

And we hope that those who experience what we've made will feel the truth of what we've shared resonate and hum within them as well. We might not even be able to put clearly into neat, descriptive prose what we've shared, but that's the beauty of art; it's not a medium that requires certainty.

As human beings, we're trying to describe what we collectively know, to create a sense of "safety in numbers" as we stare into the void together. When we reach the end of our traditional descriptive powers, it's time to weave collective meaning from poetry, painting, writing, dancing, photographing, filmmaking, storytelling, building, singing, animating, designing, baking, performing, printing, carving, sewing, sculpting, and a million other ways we daily create life out of Chaos and share it with each other for comfort.

Of course, if art is our attempt to pull Order from Chaos in the small ways we can, ultimately it's as useless as trying to plug leaks in a failing dam with our fingers. In the long run, we will fail in our attempts to hold Chaos back. Skip forward to the end of our collective story, flick through the pages to the final chapter of time, and we lose this battle. But there is something wonderfully human in the knowingly futile attempt, and no better way I can think of to spend a life.

Logos

I don't cry easily in general. When things go wrong, I go into "handle it" mode. I am the one keeping it together to find a solution in a room filled with turmoil, even if I'm experiencing the pain of the situation as keenly as everyone else. I'm the one giving out hugs to those who are crying at funerals, saving my own tears for later.

Perhaps it's my innate personality.

Perhaps it's my upbringing. My father left home when I was four years old, and I was left to hug and hold my mother as she grieved the loss of a man she loved dearly, so maybe it became a habit.

Either way, it takes a lot to make me break down over real issues.

However, I am a big softy when it comes to art.

I cried over a video game recently, believe it or not. Without giving anything away, *The Last of Us Part II* finished me off in its final scene. After spending hours with characters I really cared about, I found that the touching conclusion of the story, which offers a bittersweet moment of redemption, brought tears streaming down my face.

I always tear up when watching talented actors portray a moment of vulnerability on-screen. For example, Will Smith trying not to cry when being offered his dream job in the final scene of *The Pursuit of Happyness* always finishes me off.

Some days I get lost in "YouTube holes," watching video after video of great singers giving live performances, and I am always a blubbering mess after listening to skilled vocalists who put their heart into a song.

Most recently, I found myself quietly breaking down over an episode of the Netflix show *The Crown*, a drama following the events of the reign of Elizabeth II. Season 3, Episode 3 shows us the tragic events of the 1966 Aberfan disaster in which a colliery spoil tip on the hills above the Welsh village collapsed, killing 144 inhabitants. Most tragically, 116 of those lives claimed were of children, including 109 at the Pantglas Junior School. The building bore the brunt of the tidal wave of slurry that came careening down the hill at 9:15 a.m. on October 21, just as the kids had sat down at their desks.

The show does an amazing job of showing both the desperation and dignity of this brave community trying to mount a hopeless rescue attempt that involved digging through mounds of earth to get to their buried children with any implements they could find.

Almost a week later, on October 27, 81 children were laid to rest in a single day in a collective grave in sight of the coal tip that had taken the lives of a whole generation of that little village.

These heartbroken parents, this shattered community who were that very morning still cleaning the mud from under-neath their fingernails from digging out their children's bodies from beneath the rubble, now stood on a windswept hillside and lifted their voices, as only a Welsh choir can, and sang to a God who they had every right to be angry at.

I think I was left a lacrimal mess after watching this episode because it's true. I don't mean that the events actually happened; that's obvious. I cried because it's true that life is hard. It's true that senseless Chaos sometimes wins out. It's true that life sometimes feels purposefully cruel, as with the collapse occurring at 9:15 a.m. and not 8:15 a.m. when the children were still at home eating breakfast.

It's also true that in the face of unimaginable pain human beings can show inspiring resilience and display unbowed faith in life. It's true that sometimes in the face of overwhelming suffering the best we can do is band together and lift our voices in unison and sing.

For me, that's as good a picture as any of what we're doing when we make things. It's humanity figuratively standing on a hillside in the midst of our shared experience, banding together to sing, partly to voice our despair and partly to collectively conjure hope. But the key ingredient in all good art is that it has to tell the Truth, and I don't mean a series of dry facts.

Whereas Science tries to provide us with solutions and data, Art isn't concerned with neat answers. Art is neither careful nor certain. It isn't trying to prove anything, and it isn't certain of much. It usually isn't trying to work things out; instead, it contents itself with describing the way things are. The truth it talks about is the existential, capital "T" Truth, which we human beings intuit but can rarely voice.

Art alternately shouts and whispers through paintbrushes and typewriters, on canvases and across piano keys; it spins yarns, and arranges colours, and creates harmonies that tell us things we already sense about life but struggle to put into tidy language. Good art throws messy Truth in our faces and allows us to reel and deal with it. It's a plunge into the deep end of our lived realities.

The things we make can be positive or negative, hopeful or despairing. They can celebrate the Order or describe the Chaos, but regardless of the content, the best art rings True, and that's why it vibrates within us when we view it, taste it, hear it, or touch it.

Sometimes it's obvious what a piece is saying, like a painted portrait celebrating someone's life, which, in a museum, even comes with a little plaque beside it explaining who the subject is and why the piece was commissioned.

Sometimes we can only sense the Truth in what someone has made, like the seemingly simple blocks of colour in a Rothko painting, where everyone has a different opinion about "what it means" because it speaks different Truths to different people.

I think that on the broadest level, we're moved by created Order.

I also think we can be equally affected by created disorder, because even in the naming of Chaos, or our attempts to describe it, we are making Order from it. The most seemingly destructive and dark art that just looks like broiling Chaos from the outside is still an endeavour made at describing our experience of disorder and our collective response to it.

&

Alright, cards on the table before we go any further: in my 20s, I was a pastor.

Before you run for the hills, I promise not to try and convert you to anything. In fact, having left the institutional church a decade ago, I'm not even sure what I would try and convert you to.

That being said, I did learn a lot working for the church, and I've taken the best of what I've learned with me, including a faith that is too broad and messy for most churches to suffer but is precious to me nonetheless.

I'm going to talk about scripture for a minute, but it's important to say that I don't take it literally. In fact, personally, I think that reading ancient texts in such a fashion, especially from this time and place in history, will always rob them of their richness.

I think scripture is creativity at its best. Originally, it was spoken as poetry and stories long before it was written down, and it represents our weak and frail attempts to understand our own existence. It was set down by philosophers and theologians writing millennia before modern scientific understanding. Even before these authors put pen to paper, these stories had been making the rounds for centuries among ordinary people sitting around campfires, tending sheep and telling tales about what they thought led to the formation of everything they knew.

When you don't have answers for things, sometimes it's best to turn to art, so these people reached for vivid, poetic storytelling, which they likely never intended to be read literally. It's only the modern rational mind that insists on making that mistake. But I don't need these texts to be literally or scientifically true for them to be capital "T" True in their substance.

In both the Jewish and Christian traditions scripture begins with a picture of pure Chaos. They use the Hebrew phrase "Tohu wa-bohu," which is notoriously hard to translate, but we've given it a crack over the centuries with words like "darkness," "emptiness," "nothingness," "unseen," "void," and "formless." Safe to say the writers are suggesting that before there was "you" and "me" and "mountains" and "seas" there was nothing—proper Chaos without form.

Then these storytellers gave us this idea that God, the creative force, birthed it all in a very particular way; He "voiced" it into reality. Order came out of the "nothingness" with a spoken word.

So, in this story, there was Chaos.

Then there was a word.

Then Order.

It's very difficult to talk about this sort of thing because our rational mind jumps to creating literal pictures of an old bearded man, slightly glowing and see-through, floating in a soup of nothingness, who suddenly speaks a literal word in a booming voice; and then stars, and galaxies, and planets, and atoms, and dust, and everything else just pops into material reality.

But if we put aside that very simplistic picture and look for the nuance, there is something really profound to be mined.

There's a word theologians use for this idea of speaking Order out of Chaos: "Logos." And we get to participate in this idea through the things we make.

Logos describes the creative power of speaking Truth and wrenching goodness from calamity and meaning from mayhem. It's an intuitive voicing of the Order of things, paradoxically adding to that Order at the same time. It's speaking capital "T" Truth and creating something from nothingness in the process.

It's the lighthouse on the bluffs on a stormy night that will guide you through the turbulent waves and into the safe harbour.

It's the North Star when you are lost and confused that will help reorient you and lead you home.

In scripture, it's the light of a city on a hill at night. It's civilisation and safety in a world of uncertainty and danger.

Logos is our attempt to describe the Truth we all somehow know but struggle to articulate, because when we manage to, even in small ways, it brings us comfort and a feeling of togetherness, knowing that this experience of life—with its joys and hardships—is shared by all.

Good art is Logos.

Capital "T" Truth spoken through movements in dance, or colours on a canvas, or words on a page somehow leaves us feeling more a part of the whole and less alone. When we make things from this space, we join in that creation process in small ways; in the hearts of those who receive our work, we pull animating life out of despair.

&

If you'll allow me a little didactic dualism here—human beings use language in one of two ways.

First, we use language to elicit the response we want from the people we speak to, regardless of the veracity of what we're saying.

Second, we use language to convey the Truth, even if the results might be negative.

This choice we are faced with in language is present in the things we make as well. How do we want to use our artistic voices? Do we want to elicit a favourable response from others by playing to the crowd, or do we want to speak the Truth as we see it with the things that we make, even if the response from people isn't the one we want?

One of my favourite things to do in London is to go and sit in Room 22 at the National Gallery in Trafalgar Square. This is where they hang a selection of Rembrandt's portraits.

Now, I'm no art expert by any stretch of the imagination, and I don't know much about the techniques he used or the history of his work, but something about Rembrandt's portrait work speaks to me.

He was working at a time when painters like himself made their money by producing portraits of privileged citizens, those rich enough to commission the many hours it would take for an artist to complete a piece.

So, as an artist for hire, it would have been very tempting for him to beautify his subjects and make them look more attractive and more radiant than they perhaps were in the flesh. If he had chosen to use his substantial skill to play to the crowd, it would have led to happy customers flattered by the favourable facsimile of themselves and would, in turn, have led to a flood of referrals for future work.

So why did he die penniless, and why was he laid to rest in an unmarked grave?

Well, that's a complicated story, but perhaps in part, it's because he refused to play to the crowd. I'm not sure what the response was to his work from those who sat for his portraits, but I can't imagine that every sitter was happy. I'm a portrait photographer, and I know how sensitive some people can be about their own appearance, even when the lighting is flattering, so I can only imagine the response from the vainest of Rembrandt's sitters.

You see, his portraits are honest. They present his subjects in gritty and earthy tones. He used hard light and didn't shy away from shadows. He seemed to accentuate wrinkles in clothes and faces instead of trying to hide them. He showed his subjects as he honestly saw them—all equal victims of Time and Entropy.

He gave himself the same treatment. He is thought to have painted some 80 self-portraits over his career, some of which hang in Room 22, and if his subjects thought he was unkind to them in his portrayal, he was equally unkind to himself. His own introspective work is a searingly honest look at a man going through the ups and downs of life, and an unflinching visual diary of the ravages of time, and the toll it takes on a human face.

But when I sit and look at his portraits, I find them moving and arresting. It makes me feel something about our frailty as people, and about the beauty of our humanity being tied up in our temporary nature, and the way in which we age, and degenerate, and ultimately vanish. For me, Rembrandt is telling us capital "T" Truths through his work and not just trying to elicit favourable reviews from his customers. That's why he is remembered and why I get to sit in the National Gallery and feel comforted by the big picture he's painting. To me, his work is Logos because he tells me a difficult Truth, and it gives me comfort and internal Order in the face of our decay and decline. He offers me a hook to hang this big idea on and lets me know that we are all in the same boat, so it's ultimately OK. I'm sure it took courage, conviction, and sacrifice to make work like this, and I for one am grateful.

It's a courage I'm trying to learn in my work as well.

Portraits have always been my favourite space to work in photography. Something about the challenge of capturing an honest moment with a person, a facet of their personality, a chink in the armour that lets through a hint of who they really are has always appealed to me.

When I was starting out trying to teach myself and build a portfolio, I did what lots of photographers do: free shoots for models and actors. Whilst it's undoubtedly a great way to teach yourself the technical side of portrait photography and gather enough images to build a website, I quickly found myself getting frustrated by how "samey" the work I was producing looked. Similar faces, similar "look how sexy I am" poses, similar expressions.

I don't look down on this sort of work and I still enjoy doing it, but for myself, I knew this was now becoming more "work" and less "creativity." I needed to shake things up somehow.

So, in March of 2017, I put myself on a flight to Namibia, a country I have visited many times and that has always held a special place in my heart.

My reason for flying to the other side of the world was to take portraits with the Himba tribe, a fascinating, desert-dwelling, indigenous people native to that part of the world.

I organised a local guide and spent time with a village that was willing to host me. The approach I took was to offer photographs to those who wanted them, and instead of getting in people's faces to take images, I took the more conservative approach of setting up on the side and asking my guide to explain that if they would like photos, which I would later print and send back, they could come to where I had set up. So I spent a happy two evenings in a row taking some of the most striking portraits I had produced to date.

One quirk of shooting in this context was that I couldn't explain to my subjects that I would be taking a series of shots and choosing the best. Once they heard the camera click and saw the flash go off, they would simply walk away because I said I would take a picture, and now I had, so I must be done. I didn't want to make anyone feel uncomfortable and force them to stand there longer, so I took on the challenge of trying to get every portrait in one shot.

However, what stood out to me when taking these images was that, even though I had only one chance to get an image with most people, it was all I needed. There was no need to warm up with the camera, and there was none of the awkward "trying to find the sexy pose" that many subjects do. The Himba I spent time with had an unabashed openness, and they just stepped up to the camera and gave me the most unguarded stare and connection. There was no artifice. Just the open truth of who they were, which any portrait photographer will tell you is a gift not many are willing to give.

Reviewing those images in my tent on the night I took them made me realise I wanted more from my photography. I wanted more of this openness, no matter who I was shooting with.

So had I done it? Had I found a way to make my work more Truthful?

Well, skip forward to a few months later, when I was back in London, having decided to make some decent prints of these portraits to go on my wall at home. I headed down to one of the city's best printing houses, which prints a great deal of the exhibition photos in the UK and provides services for many Magnum photographers.

As the paper was feeding out of the machines, my images incrementally revealing themselves in lush colour, I chatted with the creative director, who was helping me that day. This guy really knew his stuff and prints work from some of the best photographers in the world. As the first image dropped onto the proofing table, I was quietly hoping he would be impressed, and in a rare moment for me, because I don't often ask for people's opinion on my work, I said, "What do you think?"

He responded, "These are technically good images of very interesting people, but I don't care about them at all."

He didn't say it unkindly, but in a moment of brutal honesty, he spun me into questioning these portraits beyond their technical proficiency. I had been caught up in the fact that I had been getting rave reviews and lavish compliments from people for these shots, but the truth was he didn't connect to them for some reason.

He went on to say that he thinks he can tell when the photographer has a connection to the work and the images mean something to them personally, and he didn't get that sense from these images.

Had I made beautiful and meaningful portraits? Or had I taken serviceable portraits of beautiful people? Were the compliments coming in because of something I had done or because of who these people were?

It took only a tiny bit of honesty with myself to know which it was. The work was Truthful, but it was the tribe's openness and Truthfulness, not mine. I realised that the creative director's comments were more than fair; they were important if I was serious about this journey. In his own act of Logos, he had given me a gift by speaking the difficult Truth to me instead of trying to please me.

Now, let me say that I don't dislike those pictures. They hang on the wall in my house and I'm still proud of them, and I'm glad I took that trip because it was a very important step on my journey. That comment that day didn't suddenly make me ashamed of them, and to be honest, I will almost certainly do more trips like this in the future because I think changing your context and subject matter regularly is essential to your growth.

But what his comments had shown me, plain as day, was that I could do better. That there was further to go and deeper to dig if I were willing to take the inward journey. I needed to find a way to speak about some capital "T" Truth that I had personally experienced.

Around this time, I heard musician John Mayer say in an interview that his songwriting is guided by a very simple mantra: "Get small, and tell the truth." That stuck with me, and I knew that whatever came next needed to be less about fancy photography techniques or finding visually compelling subjects, and more about communicating a simple and personal Truth.

So I came up with a plan. In December of the same year, I took a trip back to South Africa, where I had lived for almost 20 years. The plan was to take a series of very unfussy portraits of three men who mean a great deal to me. I travelled 1,600km, from Cape Town to Grahamstown to Durban, to photograph three mentors of mine who had been there for me in key moments of my life and stood in the gap where the lack of a present father had left a hole. The experience itself was something special and completely unlike other portrait sessions I had done.

I knew these people well and I hadn't seen them in a while, so the shoots themselves took maybe 10 minutes each. I would arrive at their houses and we would talk and catch up. I had already emailed them ahead of time, explaining what I wanted to do, so at a natural break in the conversation, I asked where it would be convenient to set up.

I used the simplest lighting possible—just a pop-up black background and one light—because I didn't want these images to be about any technical trickery. The goal was to have nothing to hide behind and to make sure that my connection with these subjects, whom I loved, could be felt in the final images.

So we talked, and laughed, and reminisced while I snapped off a few shots, and I took maybe only 30 images in total on each occasion. Then after that brief session, I packed up my gear with no break in the conversation. Normally I can get very caught up in the technical aspects of a shoot, and I would traditionally take more than 300 frames, but on these occasions, I was more interested in spending time with these men and the photography was secondary. They were the easiest shooting experiences I have ever had, bar none.

I'll admit that I was worried when leaving those sessions that I hadn't taken them seriously enough and the images would be weak as a result, but the truth is that I think they are some of the strongest images I have ever taken.

As a viewer, you can feel more of a connection to these images and me as a photographer. Even though my subjects in this series aren't as obviously striking as the shots I took of the Himba, they are stronger images because of my story with them—and this is the feedback I have received from many others, both those who know the story and those who don't.

I think it's because I love these people, and perhaps you can pick up on that when you look at them. I needed a dad, and in small ways, that's who these men were to me, even though it wasn't their job. It was pure "undeserved favour" on their part. These days the prints of those portraits hang behind me when I film videos for my YouTube channel because I like the symbolism of talking to people and sharing the things I'm learning, but I am only able to do so because of men like these who have contributed to the man I am today.

I made a short documentary about this trip and my relationship with these father figures. More than with most of the films I've made, people have reached out to share their own stories with me, especially about growing up without a father. Email after email talks fondly of the generous men who stepped in to fill the gap and helped them become good men themselves. These are existential Truths men around the world are dealing with, and by finding it in me to create portraits and a short film in which I share my own story as honestly as I can, it's provided comfort for many others who have also experienced the particular Chaos of an absent father.

&

That's Logos.

It's not a neat or easy process. So many artists will say the same thing about their work: "Sometimes I'm not sure what I'm aiming at, or exactly how to get there, but I know it when I see it." Whether we say it obliquely or directly, subtly or overtly, whether we arrive there deliberately or intuitively, art is most powerful when we are speaking the Truth with the things we make and speaking Order into the collective Chaos.

This is the art that elicits a deep response from us.

I am often brought to tears by a singer who performs a song that is clearly describing their real-life pain.

I laugh harder at a comedian who is sharing the absurdity of their story with vulnerability, where I can sense the real pathos behind the jokes.

I am moved to silence by the architecture of a masterfully designed cathedral interior that is meant to speak to the grandeur of the Divine.

I need space after experiencing a powerful film to digest the existential Truths it's nodding toward.

Something in me senses the Truth in what I'm experiencing, and even if I can't articulate why, the artist's work calls to something in me, and I feel that human connection amidst the existential mess of both our daily lives.

And I'm not happy just to be a consumer. I want to get involved. I need to create too.

It's hard to explain why, beyond the way I've stumbled through this chapter, but it has something to do with wanting to get involved with Logos. To participate. To speak the Truth of things, to join in with everyone else trying to describe, in some small measure, the way things are.

That's why, at 9 years old, I was sketching lions from my animal books.

That's why, at 15 years old, I was designing and running the lighting for our school plays.

That's why, at 20, I was fronting a band and writing music with my friends.

That's why, at 25, I was giving talks to crowds of teens and 20-somethings, trying to inspire them to be better.

That's why, at 32, I was taking copious numbers of photographs to teach myself everything I could about this evocative art form.

That's why, at 38, I was making films for my new YouTube Channel.

And that's why now, at 42, I am writing the book you are reading.

I need to create. I need to describe the Truth about life, whether it's through drawing, or singing, or songwriting, or giving speeches, or taking photographs, or making films, or writing this book. It all serves the same purpose.

All art is Logos, and when one of us gets it right, even a little bit, the rest of us feel less alone. We are figuratively holding hands, admitting we won't ultimately win our war against Entropy—and somehow that's OK.

I think that's why good art makes me cry.

Breath

I had only just turned 17 when I left high school, which seemed too young to be heading off to university straight away, so instead, I opted to take a gap year. Driven by a love for music and singing, I decided to join a music and drama group that travelled around South Africa, Namibia, and Zimbabwe for the whole year.

Now, truth be told, even though I loved singing, I was very insecure about my voice cracking. Some guys seem to sail through this awkward stage of puberty where, up until the age of 11 or so, they have the high-pitched voice of a child, and then simply wake up on their 12th birthday with the rock-solid, gravelly voice of James Earl Jones.

For some of us, though, it's a long and turbulent transition with years of voice cracks and warbles, which are embarrassing in conversation with your friends but mortally humiliating in the middle of singing a solo in front of the whole school assembly—and I'd been in that situation more than once.

So, when I joined this group, I shared with our singing coach that this was a big fear for me. His response was, "You're just not breathing right. We'll show you how."

Before we sang a note in those early classes, we were taught how to breathe—something I assumed I knew all about, seeing as I'd been involuntarily practising all my life. However, our teacher explained the physiological action of breathing in and breathing out and how most people are lazy with their breathing, and that if I wanted to sing well, I first had to learn how to breathe well.

In particular, we were taught about the diaphragm. In an early exercise, our teacher asked us to stand up straight, place our fingers against our upper stomach area, just below where the lower rib cage converges at the sternum, and breathe in deeply. For the first time in my life, I was conscious of a muscle there expanding to create a vacuum, which in turn sucked air into my lungs. Conversely, as I breathed out again it relaxed back into place and pushed air out. "Diaphragm control," he said, "is the key to singing because it will give you the column of air you need to properly support the note."

We did one fairly brutal exercise to strengthen our diaphragm muscles; we'd take a "breathing block," which was just a plank of wood maybe 15cm by 25cm, place it against our diaphragm and lean our weight against a wall. The goal was then to push ourselves away from the wall with only the muscles of our diaphragm, just by taking deep breaths in and holding the air in our lungs, and then releasing that air in a controlled and consistent stream until our lungs were empty.

We hated those breathing blocks, but they worked. I'm still sceptical as to whether that action built the muscle itself, but what those exercises definitely did was make me more aware of my own body and the muscles used to draw air into my lungs.

My voice changed after that. It still cracked occasionally but not nearly as often because the notes I sang were now more confident and better supported. I realised that all this improvement came down to setting up every note with a stronger column of air and having the control to release it smoothly. That one simple truth had unlocked my voice.

⌘

Making things is like breathing in and singing out. If the voice is the work we put out into the world, the column of air is the fuel we need to produce it.

One of our biggest quests as artists is to try to work out what our unique voice should sound like and what we uniquely have to say, but so often we forsake the in-breath we need to support that sound, so our creative voices come out as thin and reedy.

We will get to working out what our unique creative voice is in the next chapter, but first, we have to spend some time on the oft-neglected but crucial in-breath.

Some common complaints I hear are:

"I love to make things, but I just don't know what to make."

"I've bought a camera, but I don't know what to take photographs of."

"I want to write short stories, but I have no idea what they should be about."

I think the simple answer for our lack of direction or motivation is that we're trying to speak without first taking a breath. We have to learn to put first things first.

This isn't a problem confined to the beginners amongst us, either. Veteran artists of many years can still regularly hit that point where they have all the skill and experience necessary to create beautiful things but no idea what to point those abilities at. Like the air we breathe, we need to draw in our energies, our message, our ideas, even our motivation to make new things.

The word "inspiration" is an interesting one when you break it down. It comes to us fairly unaltered from the Latin word "inspiratio" which literally means "drawing in of breath," or "being breathed into by the Divine."

The Greeks used the word "Pneuma" which did double duty as a word describing both "spirit" and "breath." The Stoics, in particular, used the same word to describe the life-giving, animating spirit, or creative force within human beings.

In the same way, a derivative of our English word "spirit" hides in the middle of our word for breathing, "respiration."

Language links like this betray the notion that human beings for thousands of years seem to have intuited a connection between "creativity," "inspiration," "spirit," and a "Divine in-breathing."

The Greeks even went so far as to anthropomorphize this creative source in the form of "the Muses," suggesting that all creative flow came from this pantheon of goddesses with names like Calliope, the Muse of Epic Poetry; Euterpe, the Muse of Music; and Thalia, the Muse of Comedy.

These ideas have carried over into our modern day as well in a number of guises. I remember when working for the church that it was common parlance to suggest that you were "guided by the Holy Spirit" when writing a song or delivering a sermon.

Even in secular culture, artists have adopted flesh-and-blood human beings as their tangible muses—people who have become regular "subjects" for their paintings, poems, or songs. These artists suggest that their work gains a vitality from the transfer of energy, spirit, or pneuma simply because they spend regular time in the presence of their chosen muses.

I suppose what this all suggests to me is that when we make, we are looking to be inspired, in-spired, breathed-in to in order to receive everything we need to create.

How many times have we sat staring at blank canvases and blank pages, frustrated that nothing seems to be flowing, wondering if the Muses have forsaken us? Is it maybe because we are trying to speak out, before taking a deep breath in?

So how do you take a creative in-breath? Well, I think it comes down to creating space for ourselves, without agenda.

Have you ever noticed that you seem to get your best ideas in the shower? I think the reason is simple. We live at a time when we are constantly filling our faces with stimuli designed to keep us distracted. We always have a screen of some sort in front of us, whether it's our computer, our phone, or the TV, and we are constantly taking in a seemingly never-ending stream of information and entertainment.

But when you hop in the shower, it's just you. For a few minutes, you are alone, nothing but the sound of water falling, and there is often a moment when you just relax, close your eyes, and enjoy the sensation. It's one of the rare moments most of us take to be properly alone and quiet in our modern world. In my experience, it's in these "empty moments" that the brain starts to generate ideas. Is there something to learn from this that we can replicate more often?

If we think about these quiet moments in our day and the generative mental space they spark, then surely the trick is just to re-create these spaces more often. If we are feeling uninspired and directionless we need to learn to move things out of the way long enough for our mind to do what it does best: form new ideas.

But there is a trap laid for us straight away the minute we understand this principle, and it's the reason I used the phrase "without agenda" above. There is a kind of borderless free-thinking that happens when we create that empty mental space for ourselves, and I think the reason it generates ideas and gives us inspiration is that we aren't thinking within the narrow confines we usually do when we are more actively directing our thoughts.

How often has there been a problem you've needed to solve in your life, and you've sat for hours, anxiously mulling it over, hoping to come up with a solution, but nothing new arrives? We even use phrases like "racking my brain" to describe the repetitive mental torture we put ourselves through to force a solution.

Later, you might find yourself taking a walk, not really paying attention, and the solution just effortlessly presents itself in a eureka moment. You weren't even aware that you were specifically processing the issue, but the solution is suddenly there. When we are stressed about feeling stuck, we sometimes try and force a resolution and our conscious minds push thoughts through the same well-worn channels, expecting a different result. However, when we stop trying to compel the solution through our conscious minds and allow our unconscious to have a crack at finding a way forward, our brains can move in more supple and creative ways to come up with new ideas.

The trap I'm talking about is that we could understand this principle and take longer walks, or meditate, or take a couple of days away to get in-spired, but if we go with an agenda, we are still in our conscious minds. If we take a couple of hours to go and sit by ourselves but are aware that the only reason we are doing so is that we need to find inspiration, that hyper-awareness of the problem we are trying to solve will keep us from empty, generative space. We will be pulling ourselves out of those quiet moments, restlessly checking if we had a new idea, worried about "whether it's working," impatient for "results."

It just doesn't work like that. The space we take has to be without agenda, and it should be an ongoing lifestyle choice and not a gimmick we use only in response to those moments when we feel as if we've hit a dead end. You have to make creating agendaless mental space a regular practice for it to work.

Another common problem is that a lot of us fear being alone and quiet. It makes us very uncomfortable.

Perhaps there are parts of ourselves we are running from that always seem to surface when we're alone.

Perhaps memories from our past haunt us.

Perhaps we use the social noise of good company, or a multiplicity of stimuli, to avoid ourselves and the things we don't want to deal with.

Perhaps this explains the pervasive addiction to our mobile phones, which habitually come out of our pockets when we are left alone, even for a few seconds. No judgement intended here; I do exactly the same thing, and I have to call myself on when I am drowning out those empty moments from my life.

Every artist of any stripe needs to start by dealing with their issues and making friends with themselves so that space becomes not only tolerable but desirable. That's really the only way to avoid becoming the clichéd tortured artist who can't create because they're uninspired and their demons won't leave them alone. If our goal is to make beautiful things, it's a journey we have to take.

I'm not telling you anything human beings haven't known for millennia. Virtually every tradition and culture around the world knows the value of making space for yourself.

Native American teens were sent alone into the wilderness to fast and face themselves, to listen, and to come back to the community to deliver a vision that would hopefully benefit all.

The Naga Sadhus live naked and covered in ash, separated from society along the banks of the Ganges, and people from all over the world travel to seek them out and learn what they've heard in the empty space they've carved out for themselves.

We have stories of the emperors of China seeking out hermits who had withdrawn to the wilderness, to listen to their counsel and hear from a truly generative mind.

Christian ascetics sought out remote desert caves and rocky coastal islands as locations to separate themselves from the noise of daily life and to be better able to hear from God.

Jesus himself is recorded to have walked into the desert for 40 days and nights to fast, be alone, and face his demons before he began his teaching work. He knew he needed to be breathed-in to first.

It seems clear that we all intuitively know that people who create space have more important things to tell the rest of us. When we've breathed in, when we are in-spired, we often come away with something to share that others may have missed in the mad rush of daily life, and that can only enrich the things we make.

Now I'm not suggesting you need to disappear into the wilderness—although don't let me stop you. Personally, I want to keep living the life I have, but all this reminds me that I can never allow my life to become too busy or too noisy if I am serious about having good things to say with the things I make. I can't complain about feeling uninspired if I haven't stopped and taken intentional space for myself, because the cause and the solution are both painfully obvious.

The Muses don't run after us, throwing fresh ideas and inspiration at us while we are running off in the other direction, filling our faces with distracting stimuli. They demand that we stop and create generative space and quiet before they will give their gifts. We can't get around it.

&

I have just a couple of basic practices that I make sure to fit into my life.

The first is that I take retreats.

A couple of times a year, I try and get away by myself, even just for a few days. I'm not travelling around the world and staying in fancy hotels, partly because I can't justify spending a load of money on these trips, but mostly because I think retreats are best done simply. I might book a little cabin somewhere remote, with few modern conveniences, to reduce distractions. Solo camping or hiking is a great way to retreat as well. The point is just to get away from what's familiar, to change your setting and create space for yourself.

The second is that I walk a lot.

You don't have to invest huge amounts of time in taking space; you just have to do a little bit regularly. I understand that taking a retreat is a luxury for many people, and requires an investment of time or money you may not be able to afford at the moment, but taking a walk? Surely that's something all of us can do.

I have a friend who talks about taking "micro-holidays." If things are getting overwhelming for her in a day, she might just go sit in a coffee shop for half an hour with a book, and that is her micro-holiday: time set aside—no matter how brief—to escape and refresh. My favourite micro-holiday is taking myself on a walk; it's my go-to way to create some silence and hear from the Muses.

What is the idea of pilgrimage, after all, if not a very long walk, with a healthy dose of solitude, to face ourselves and hear new things? Obviously, each religious tradition has their own emphasis and content, but whether you are walking the road to Mecca or the Camino de Santiago in Spain, or strolling down the Thames in London on a Sunday afternoon, the root practice holds the same basic idea; human beings worked out a long time ago that a good walk and some alone time can shake new things loose.

&

No matter how you choose to take space, there is one very practical tip I can give you, and it's one that everyone who practices any form of meditation will already know: focus on your breathing.

Before you think I'm about to get all woo-woo on you and sign you up to some cult or get you to pay a guru for your custom mantra, I don't think the various trappings that have developed around meditation are that important. The fact that every form of spirituality seems to practice some version of the same method suggests to us that this is a universal human practice and isn't owned by any one group.

The reason for focusing on your breathing isn't a magical one but rather a pragmatic one. Our minds will try to pull us into the future where we are worried about the next set of bills, or into the past where someone wronged us. But generative mental space, the fertile soil for new ideas, requires that we stay in an empty and open present. So when your mind pulls you away, you need something happening in that open "now" to pull you back when your conscious mind inevitably wanders. Well, seeing as you have to breathe anyway, why not focus on that?

The rise and fall of your chest.

The sensation of air entering and exiting your lungs.

The feeling of being alive, of respirating.

"Re-in-spirating" if you like.

I don't want to promise you that every time you create this kind of space for yourself you will be flooded with ideas because that would be dishonest, but I will say this: the vast majority of my better creative ideas and inspiration have surfaced during times when I've closed down the noise of my conscious mind and allowed my subconscious to take over.

It might have been a walk.

It might have been a retreat I took for a few days.

It might have been 10 minutes in the shower.

However we choose to do it, we have to learn how to creatively breathe in.

&

Not all in-spiration comes from creating empty space, though. Another essential way to keep our ideas flowing is to consume the works of others like fuel. By enjoying those creative voices around us and hearing their spoken Logos, we will be changed and inspired to speak our own big "T" Truths as well.

I'm a big believer that what you put in is what you get out. What you put in will turn you into someone, will open your mind in particular ways, will give you things to say, and will shape how you see the world. So many of us, when starting out in any art form, spend our time learning techniques that feel like quick wins, and of course, there is nothing wrong with that. We need to become technically proficient and work on the skills of our chosen medium. But we also have to balance that time spent teaching ourselves techniques with saturating ourselves in the works of other artists.

For example, I've been taking regular breaks from writing this book to sit down and read, especially when I feel stuck. The books I'm choosing to read have nothing to do with this subject matter, but just the act of inhaling writing from others helps me to exhale my own.

Inspiration is infectious.

Photographers, how many times have you looked at a great image from another photographer, and it's driven you to grab your camera and go out because your understanding of what's possible has suddenly been expanded?

And "soaking" in the things others have made need not be limited to the art form we are engaged in. There have been poems inspired by paintings, songs inspired by stories, films inspired by photographs, and everything in between. We shouldn't limit ourselves, but we need to be deliberate about how we consume, because if we're not careful, we will just be back to fighting against distracting noise.

What we make will come out of who we are, and the work that inspires us will shape us. That's why I take developing myself, my mind, and my worldview very seriously, because my photography, my filmmaking, and my writing come out of who I am and how I see. More than that, I want to be an interesting, interested, awake, and aware human being for my own sake, and taking in the works of other "makers of things" has contributed to who I am in ways I will likely never fully understand.

So I consider myself an autodidact, which is just a fancy word for someone who takes responsibility for constantly teaching themselves new things. I'm a self-teacher.

To be very honest with you, I was no high-flying student in high school. I scraped through my final exams in South Africa, many on Standard Grade (which involved easier tests and exams). I was endlessly frustrated that education seemed to be more a test of short-term memory than anything else. However, when I left formal education and I could suddenly read whatever book I wanted to because there was no book report due, an exciting possibility opened up to me. I could design my own curriculum for life learning.

I gave myself books to read about subjects that really interested me, like history and the biographies of people who moved society forward. I read books on spirituality, philosophy, and psychology to learn how we are wired as a species and how we've tried to answer the big questions. I read books on mythology because I believe that by understanding the stories humans have been telling since we began recording them, we can also understand what we care about; and hopefully, in turn, I can begin to speak about these things with the work I make.

You might be surprised from that list that as a photographer I don't read a lot of photography books, but I feel that the books I choose to read offer a more deliberate way of pursuing my fascination with people and their ideas, drives, and beliefs. Hopefully, as I fill my head with this stuff, I'll gain perspective and direction for my camera. It will be in-spiring.

I understand that reading isn't for everyone. I'm assuming that's not you because we're interacting now through this book, but I've become more convinced of the importance of reading over the last decade. More than any other medium, reading has expanded my worldview and taught me how to see more clearly.

A couple of years ago, I did an online filmmaking course with the inimitable Werner Herzog. As part of the course, he recommended one particular book. You might assume that it would have been a hefty tome on the history of filmmaking or a bumper manual on filmmaking methodology, but in fact, it was a fairly obscure book called *The Peregrine*, by J. A. Baker. First published in 1967, the entire book simply describes in beautiful prose the peregrine falcons which were native to the wilds of Essex at the time Baker lived there. Herzog makes the point that this man's descriptive powers over this singular subject are phenomenal but that he is able to write this way only because he has first learnt to see.

Herzog starts the course by intoning in his mesmeric Bavarian accent, "My best advice to all filmmakers is to read, read, read, read, read, read, read."

Incidentally, the first exercise he gives the class is "to walk 100 miles in any direction." That's it. Don't film it, or photograph it, just walk it. This is a man who decided to walk from Munich to Paris in 1974 to see his dying mentor, Lotte Eisner. There were plenty of modes of transport available to him, but he chose to walk it with just a compass and a duffel bag in the middle of winter, and that journey, among many others, taught him to see and helped make him the filmmaker he is today. He wrote a beautiful diary on the journey that was later published as *Of Walking in Ice* if you want to dig a little deeper.

If I needed reminding—and I often do—it was all there in Herzog's course: reading, walking, learning to see, creating space.

Another medium that features heavily in the curriculum I've built for myself is film. Masterful directors have taught me about visual storytelling and pacing. My favourite cinematographers have shown me work that sparks endless ideas for my own. The better scriptwriters have taught me about life and people in ways psychology never could, because they've made me feel the Truth of who we are, beyond the science. Their work helps me become a better filmmaker, photographer, and storyteller, so I regularly select films that may require more patience and concentration but that I know will open me up to new possibilities.

I also consume podcast interviews with interesting human beings because their ideas about life challenge my own and force me to see through the eyes of others.

I visit museums. I'll be candid and say that I often don't stay long. Personally, if I know I will have access to the space again, I will likely just visit one or two rooms and leave, and come back on another day to try a few more; otherwise, I know I will just hit a saturation point and stop taking in what I'm seeing. You've already heard in the last chapter that the Rembrandt room in the National Gallery is a particular favourite of mine.

I love listening to live music, though not necessarily big gigs in stadiums or arenas; my favourites are singer-songwriters who strip everything down and just deliver their Logos in song.

You will have a different list from mine, but the point is to design your own curriculum that feeds you with art that will broaden your perspective. So cultivate curiosity and breathe it all in because I promise you it will provide the creative column of air you need and form the wellspring of ideas from which your best creative work will flow. Spending agendaless time in your own company will help you get to know yourself better and what you uniquely have to offer; and knowing more about the world you live in can only help you better understand what it means to be human and will enable you to speak Logos to us through your unique gifts.

This is all the creative in-breath. The in-spiration. You can't skip it, because as my singing coach always used to say, "You can't sing a note unless you've drawn in enough air to support it first."

Maybe you need to take yourself on longer walks or more solo coffee dates. Maybe you need to get away for a few days, a few weeks, a few months. You'll have to make friends with yourself. You'll have to get comfortable with empty space, but I promise you, your creative endeavours will flourish if you make the effort.

If you learn to be still.

Just to be.

Just breathe.

Voice

The other day I called my bank for some boring administrative reason, and right from the start of the call, the gentleman on the other end just seemed overly chatty. He didn't want to let me get straight to the business I had called him for and kept asking me questions about the weather, and politics, and how I enjoyed life in London.

I started to feel sorry for him. I thought about how tedious his job must be and how sitting in an office on the phone all day might be quite isolating, so I decided I would give him some time and be patient with the fact that he was obviously just happy for the chance to talk to somebody about something other than bank balances and interest rates.

But in the middle of patting myself on the back for being such a long-suffering and compassionate human being, he suddenly cut me off and said, "Thank you Mr. Tucker. I can confirm you have passed voice identification."

I suddenly realised that he wasn't interested in talking to me at all; he was just doing his job. He was keeping me talking so my voice could be identified by the computer on his end and confirm that I was who I said I was.

That's how unique human voices are. We have taught computers to be able to positively identify me from you and the billions of other human beings on the planet, just by listening to my distinctive patterns of speech. In fact, my accent, cadence, resonance, and intonation are so unrepeatable that my bank is happy to use it as a form of positive identification.

I find the human voice fascinating. We all draw air into our lungs using the same biological mechanism. The process looks the same and mostly sounds the same, but the moment we push that air through our vocal cords, suddenly there are endless varieties of the human voice.

You have a unique tone and timbre to your voice, a register and resonance all your own.

Your age shapes your voice over time.

Your biological sex will influence its pitch.

Your language and culture will dictate the shape of sounds that come easily to you, while your locale will craft an accent that frames the way you speak.

Even your personality will play a role in things like the volume, pace, and intensity of the way you use your voice.

In the same way, you have a unique creative voice to give to the world through the things you make. While the journey can be a long and messy one, you've taken that creative in-breath, so now it's time to discover what that voice sounds like.

⌂

Let me tell the story of how I discovered an aspect of my own creative voice.

I began shooting street photography at a time when my day job was creatively frustrating. I was working as a photographer, but my 9-to-5 job was shooting sofas for an e-commerce website. That meant that most of my time was spent in cold warehouses photographing up to 50 sofas a day, each from exactly the same six angles to give the website a consistent look.

My time spent with a camera in hand had become so technical and repetitive that I didn't like picking it up anymore, and that worried me. I initially started down this road fuelled by an excitement around photography, and I could tell that if I didn't do something drastic I was well on my way to giving up on this art form altogether.

So I decided to give myself a simple photography project, on the side of my day job, to keep my love of this medium alive.

I didn't have a lot of extra time, but I realised that I walked 30 minutes to and from the station every day on my commute, and that added up to an hour that I could be using for more than just travel. So I gave myself a challenge; I would use that daily walk to take photos of the things I saw with the goal of capturing at least one image a day that I was happy with.

I deliberately kept the exercise as loose as possible. This was meant to be untechnical, messy, reactive creativity because I needed something to balance out the rigid way I had to use cameras, lights, and composition for my day job. I even chose to use my phone camera instead of my fancy work camera because it gave me more permission to play, letting me take myself less seriously. I didn't beat myself up about perfect exposure or framing; I just took images intuitively as I strolled along. That simple little task rescued me from walking away from the camera altogether and brought me back to the creative possibilities of making photographs.

In fact, I enjoyed it so much that I started to spend time on weekends heading out to see how good I could get if I leaned into the well-established genre of street photography. But I immediately faced an issue. On a couple of occasions, I was approached by people who asked what I was taking photos of. They weren't familiar with the law in the UK and the freedom it gives street photographers, so they became pretty combative, suggesting that I wasn't allowed to take photos of people and scenes out in public, and they were going to call the police.

In both cases, I was able to diffuse the situation by staying calm and friendly, pulling up website links to show them what UK law said, and explaining how street photography is a long-standing art form that is perfectly legal in this little corner of the world. However, those confrontations left a bitter taste in my mouth. I realised that traditional street photography draws a very particular personality type, and as an introvert, this might not be a good fit for me.

I remember one day in particular that highlighted my reticence toward this genre. I was out taking photos with a photographer friend of mine named Ondrej, and we had just been through Soho and Chinatown in London and decided to head down to Trafalgar Square. The scene greeting us when we arrived was a surreal one. The place was absolutely packed. Sunderland football fans, many of them fairly inebriated, had taken over the whole space and were celebrating by singing songs, waving flags, jumping into the fountains, and hoiking footballs high into the air.

Now, I should probably say that when Ondrej isn't shooting street photography, he is taking himself off to war zones to shoot images of frontline conflict, so nothing about the chaos we had stumbled upon put him off in the slightest. In fact, his eyes lit up as we approached, and in seconds he was darting in and out of the crowd and grabbing shots of drunk revellers tussling and jostling with each other, even being rewarded with a football to the face from close range for his troubles.

Despite complaining that his camera got a big jolt and that he couldn't feel the left side of his face, he was grinning from ear to ear and had some interesting images to show for his efforts. I, on the other hand, had gotten no shots. It was entirely my fault too because I was skirting the edge of the crowd the whole time, watching from the sidelines, too intimidated to get stuck in like Ondrej, and trying instead to get compelling shots from safer vantage points, which of course was never going to work.

You see, I don't like crowds. As an introvert, being in loud, congested spaces, or having confrontations with people who take offence to photographers working in public, takes me far from my happy place.

When it comes to finding out what your creative voice is, it's really important to pay attention to these moments. We are often looking for the times we feel things are clicking and we're doing work that makes us happy, but it's also crucial to acknowledge those moments when we feel we're having to push against the grain of our personality to get anything done. Maybe it's a sign that this direction isn't for us, or that we need to step outside the confines of the traditional art form we're engaged with and do something different with it—something that flows easier from who we are as individuals.

That's what I did after that. I didn't give up on street photography; I just stopped trying to take the images I thought everyone expected me to make and started to take the photos that felt right to me. I'll admit that at the start the process was very intuitive. I just followed my gut and photographed what interested me. I began to notice that I was actually drawn more toward the shapes made by hard light and shadow than the people who were out and about. The human beings in my frames started to get smaller and smaller and served to provide a sense of scale for the scene rather than feature as the main focal points of my images.

One of the ancillary reasons I had stumbled onto this style of shooting was that it negated potential conflict. If I ran around like more traditional street photographers who shoot individual subjects, then people would rightly ask questions as to what I was doing. However, I had found a focus for my images that didn't look for people first; I was looking for interesting spaces and light. I would find a compelling composition and wait to see who came through. People would still notice me taking photos, but the response was different now. When they saw me, they didn't ask, "Hey, did you just take my photo?" Instead, they'd say, "I'm so sorry I walked in the way of your shot," just because I was there before they were. I had found a way to exchange confrontation for an apology, which I could just play off with something jovial like, "Don't worry about it. I was waiting for you," and after a giggle, they would move on.

The more I photographed and listened to my intuition, the more a loose style began to coalesce. I was playing with high contrast, exposing for the highlights and letting the shadows in my images fall to black. I toyed with the shapes cast as sunlight and architecture collided, and I often positioned the humans in my shots so that their faces were obscured in shadow. My visual voice was emerging one shutter click at a time.

It wasn't traditional street photography.

It wasn't anything like the New York City street tableaus of Joel Meyerowitz.

It wasn't like the strobe-lit street portraits of Bruce Gilden.

It bore no resemblance to Fred Herzog's careful visual study of Vancouver in the 1950s.

Street photographers can be a snobbish bunch, and I was told early on that I had drifted too far from the tradition to legitimately call this more abstract work "street photography" because even though it was shot on the street, the subject matter didn't fit the definition somehow.

A part of me wondered if I was too far off-piste and whether I was being self-indulgent. Had following my gut led me astray?

But then the work of two artists, whom I will sadly never meet because they have both passed away, gave me permission to keep walking in the direction I was going.

The first was Fan Ho.

I had never heard of him until I started to share the work I was making online, and a few people commented that what I was doing reminded them of Fan Ho's work, so I looked him up.

Fan Ho was a Chinese photographer and filmmaker probably most famous in photography circles for the work he did on the streets of Hong Kong in the 1950s and 1960s. When I did that initial online search to find out who everyone was talking about, I remember being immediately struck by his work. His photography was obviously a lot more refined than mine, but I felt a familiarity with what he was doing. He also loved to play with hard light in his images, and his subjects were often backlit and anonymous.

There was a real comfort in knowing someone else had already trodden this path I was on: looking for shapes in the light and shadow and using people for context rather than making them the identifiable subject of the image. His work gave me permission to keep going. It told me that I wasn't crazy or that far off the map. In fact, the work I was doing wasn't even new, a discovery that led to a healthy sense of humility. We all stand on the shoulders of giants, and my job now was to keep exploring and pushing to define my own voice in this well-worn vein.

The second artist was Edward Hopper.

Similarly, his name kept popping up in comments under the images I was making, and it was time to dispel my ignorance of this artist too. After looking him up, I discovered that Hopper was an American Realist painter most famous for his work in oils. He sought to depict urban life in the 1950s in the U.S. and did so in his own inimitable style.

He also loved to replicate hard light and shadow in his work, and he would often paint a lonely figure in a lot of space.

A single occupant at a table in a cafe staring thoughtfully into her cup of tea.

A businessman sitting alone at a desk gazing out of the office window, in quiet reverie.

A woman taking a moment for herself in a theatre hallway as the movie plays in the background.

Surely, if you're going to feature city life, it should involve crowds of people and the manic bustle of metropolitan existence, right? So why did he choose to depict isolated subjects who feel very alone and cut off? Was he saying something about how many of us feel in these settings?

In addition to his familiar use of light, his focus on isolated subjects opened things up further, helping me realise what I'd been intuitively moving toward, as many of my images also featured single individuals alone in the city.

Sometimes, as makers of things, our direction and intention are clear to us. However, the rest of the time we rely on a gut feeling and have to work out what we're doing as we go. As I hinted at in the previous chapter, this is where breathing-in the works of other artists can help us unlock our own voice, and in my case, Ho and Hopper both posthumously helped a floundering photographer work out what he was already trying to say, by responding to the Logos in their work and connecting to the unique ways they saw and captured the world.

As I looked at Fan Ho's use of composition and shadow and Hopper's repeated exploration of isolated subjects in urban spaces, I suddenly realised what I was trying to say in my own way.

I live in one of the busiest cities in the world, and the rush of city life has never sat well with me. Born in the UK, but having grown up in Africa, culturally I didn't feel at home when I returned a few years ago; there was definitely an adjustment period.

Most British men my age choose to spend their days socialising in crowded pubs arguing about their football teams, but I couldn't care less about sports, I'm not a big drinker, and I don't like noisy spaces where you have to yell over the top of each other to be heard. I never have.

I prefer a quiet cafe and a one-on-one chat.

I choose the table in the quietest corner.

I love an empty park.

I plan my route to avoid the busy thoroughfares and choose the emptier streets instead.

I enjoy sitting in a vacant church for 15 minutes when I have a little time to kill.

I like a bench on a hill above the noise of the city.

That's where you'll find me.

I'm that guy.

This means that I am often walking around on my own, watching the crowds from the sidelines, and at different points in my life that left me feeling alone and on the outside of things.

But, over time, I made friends with this part of myself, and rather than viewing it as a failing of some sort, I came to like that I was wired this way. In fact, that's the person I saw in Fan Ho's images and in Hopper's paintings. Their work was a mirror for me, and in turn, it helped me realise what I was doing in my own work. My camera had become a sort of therapy; a tool of self-discovery. It's this quieter aspect of my personality that made me gravitate toward isolated subjects in my images, solitary people moving through light and shadow in big city spaces. I see them because I see myself in them.

Perhaps more than that. Perhaps I was photographing my own sense of isolation being in a city yet feeling somehow separate from the goings-on.

An observer.

A watcher.

Someone moving alone, along the periphery.

A single figure walking in the liminal spaces where light and shadow meet.

In a very real sense, taking images of the things I was drawn to, combined with discovering the works of Ho and Hopper, and a bit of self-awareness, helped me realise that I was actually taking images of myself. I was using my creative voice to offer images reflecting my own experience of life in the city I live in. Just the act of creating these images gives me a feeling of Order in the Chaos of life in London, and in offering that Logos to others, I hope to provide some recognition and comfort for people who experience metropolitan life in the same way I do.

I'm not naive enough to assume that everyone would read this in the images I make. After all, it's taken me years to realise it myself. Most just enjoy the aesthetics, but for those willing to dig a little deeper, they might pick up on the capital "T" Truth I'm sharing.

You see, I think it's in the mix of all these things that our unique creative voices emerge. Artists make a common mistake, especially when starting out, of thinking that individual style, or creative voice, comes from our chosen technique or the tools we choose to use. We have to avoid wasting too much time on these things and get to the bigger questions as early on in our creative journeys as we can; otherwise, we are in real danger of getting stuck "majoring on minors."

Whether Hopper had chosen to paint in oils, watercolours, or acrylics, his paintings would have still looked like his. They would have had his unique visual signature and his message baked into them no matter what technique he had settled on.

Whether Ho had chosen to shoot with a Leica or a Voigtländer, a 35mm or a medium-format camera, his images would still have looked like his because tools and techniques don't supply you with your creative voice.

That's hard internal work that can't be bought at a camera store or learnt in an online tutorial.

ở

So how do you discover your own creative voice?

Honestly, I don't believe there is one neat road there, but I can give you some practical exercises that have worked for me.

The first is to create a lot. There is no substitute for this step. Laziness, or more likely, fear of failure, can keep us stuck on the sofa hoping to will a fully formed aesthetic into our creative minds that we can go out and flawlessly execute on from day one, but deep down we know that's not how it works. We can only discover our creative voice by making— and making a lot.

My journey to developing a voice with the images I was taking out on the streets, although it took me only a few pages to walk you through it, has taken five years, hundreds of hours, and tens of thousands of images to discover, and it's far from clear to me still, even to this day. I expect it will take a great deal more shooting before I truly feel that I have discovered my creative voice in this space. All I have at the moment is a loose direction and a long road ahead of me, and for now, that's enough.

That's why Henri Cartier-Bresson is famously quoted as saying, "Your first 10,000 photographs are your worst." He's letting us know that if we want to develop it's going to take hours and hours of doing that thing we love, and potentially doing it badly, in order to work out what we have to say and how we want to say it. There is no shortcut for doing.

None of it is wasted time either. Make no mistake; it can be really frustrating because we often feel more competent than we are, and those days where nothing seems to be working tempt us to give up altogether. However, even on those days when we feel as if we're just making a mess and getting nowhere, we are actually discovering what our voice doesn't sound like, and that is as much a part of the process. We might be working out what sort of things we don't want to say, or what things we are just making because we imagine other people expect them of us. All this is as important as the days when we make big discoveries in the affirmative about our own creative voices. In fact, I would go so far as to say those big days never come without 100 frustrating days of experimentation beforehand.

The second suggestion is to pay attention to your gut. Intuition is going to be a better guide than your rational mind, which is why we spoke about the importance of creating space for your unconscious mind to process. Use your instincts to discern between the things you're drawn to and the things that don't fit. Learn to eschew the expectations of others and to follow your instincts even if you're not sure where they will lead, even if you make a mess with your work for a while. If there is something new to be born in your work, the only way to deliver it is by following that inner instinct. You don't have to show anyone what you're doing yet if you aren't happy with the work you are producing, but you do have to give yourself permission to explore where your gut is leading, even if you don't understand it yet. Understanding often comes later. For now, trust your gut.

The third is to look at the work of other artists and identify what connects. As we've already said, it doesn't have to be directly related to the work you're doing. It could be photography or film, poetry or music, painting or writing, but it's important to pay attention to the work that speaks to you in any and every genre and ask yourself what resonates within you.

What is it about their unique voice that speaks to you?

Do they talk about things you care about?

Do they affirm your own worldview in some way, and how can you take that affirmation and apply it to your own work?

For me, Ho and Hopper, a fellow photographer and a painter, respectively, were keys to unlocking a part of my creative voice. They had already blazed this particular trail in their own ways, and I was grateful they had gone ahead of me because the going was now easier as I followed.

It's worth saying that this isn't about copying the voice of other artists in place of your own voice. We all start out by following our heroes and trying to replicate their work; it's how we learn in the beginning, but we do ourselves a great disservice if we remain in that creatively childish space for too long. If we do, we run the risk of being nothing more than a faint echo of what someone else has achieved, instead of achieving something for ourselves. There is nothing wrong with rooting yourself in your heroes' work at the beginning and even allowing their voice to reverberate through you until your own voice emerges, but remember that the purpose is always to uncover your own unique voice. So, for your own sake, I hope you will move from imitation to innovation as quickly as possible.

Bigger than all these suggestions, though, you have to get to know yourself. That authentic space inside each of us is where all good art comes from. I know "authentic" is an overused word these days but no synonym quite captures that mix of honest, genuine, and personal.

We are attracted to that which we sense is real, something created without artifice and offered vulnerably. We may be impressed with a single piece of work from any artist, but the artists we choose to follow into the future are those who have given us a little bit of themselves.

It's the songwriters who bare a bit of their soul whom we fall in love with.

It's the authors who share their stories with an unabashed openness of whom we say, "I will read anything they write."

It's the filmmakers creating stories that mirror their own lives and experiences—like Quentin Tarantino's visual references to the old cinema he loves—who we champion. The passion he exudes is genuine and personal, and we can feel it as we watch.

When we pick up that an artist is making something to communicate Truth as they see it and they aren't putting on a persona just to impress the masses, it's that vulnerability that hooks us in.

But they have to know themselves well to do that—and perhaps even like themselves to some extent, flaws and all. Maybe that's why we find this sort of work so compelling—because we find the human being behind it so inspiring in their openness and honesty. We want that for ourselves, and we know that it's a tough journey to reach that level of personal development and acceptance.

In our chapter on Logos, I told you about a series of portraits I took of my mentors, but it took a long time before I was ready to take those images and talk about the story behind them on film.

I've been to hours of therapy over the years. I began when I was studying psychology and we were told that every good psychologist is in regular therapy themselves. Even though I never practised as a psychologist, I still decided to take that suggestion and whenever I could afford it—regardless of whether I was navigating a crisis—I made sure to attend some sessions for myself. I think it's helpful for all of us to sit with someone objective who can act as a mirror for us. If they are good at their job they can call out the convenient lies we tell ourselves and help us to see our blind spots.

I remember years ago talking to a therapist about how I was struggling in my job. I didn't have a good relationship with my boss and found him very intimidating. If I'm honest, I found all older men scary and even struggled to look them in the eye when they spoke to me. She began to dig, as therapists are wont to do, and we ended up discussing my past and how my father had left home when I was four years old. She turned to me and said, "You need to be a little kinder to yourself. You didn't grow up with a male authority figure in your life, and so they are strange and frightening beings to you. You need to start by realising the hole your father left, and then with that new awareness and an understanding that older men are just people too, work out how you can build some healthy relationships with the male authority figures in your life."

Without this realisation, I wouldn't have had male mentors in my life because I wouldn't have had the grace to accept them. I certainly wouldn't have had the inclination to take those portraits of those precious men, or the ability to tell the story behind them if I hadn't owned my story and my issues. I needed to forgive everyone involved, myself included, before I could even begin to talk about or create around it.

We have to get to know ourselves first.

I've already shared the biographical details about my birth and upbringing and my career in the church, and some of the impact these experiences have had on who I am today. I'm also a Type One with a Two-Wing on the Enneagram Personality Test and an INFJ on the Myers-Briggs Type Indicator, which means I am an introvert who values truth and honesty above all things. This can lead to a tendency to see things as black and white, which can feel rigid to those who deal with me, and I need to be aware of when this surfaces in the things I make.

I am creative, insightful, and inspiring, but I can also be overly sensitive and a brutal perfectionist. I'm an idealist at heart and believe the best about human beings, but that also means that I can expect too much from people, and some days, the pain of the world weighs heavily on me.

This is who I am and how I'm wired. Everything I make will come out of who I am. My creative voice springs from my personality, my upbringing, the things I've seen, my story, and the worldview it's all conspired to give me. My job is to make things, from my story outwards, with my unique creative voice as I wield my camera, or my pen, or my spoken words. The goal is to speak the capital "T" Truth as I've experienced it in my life, with my creative accent, intonation, resonance, and inflexion. All this is why the in-breath is so crucial—because it's in this space that we learn who we are and incorporate the things we've seen and experienced into the things that we make.

&

So who are you?

What do you care about?

What is your story and how has it shaped the way you see the world?

What do you want to tell the world about it, and how can you begin to weave that message into your creative work? There is nothing wrong with trying to work out what your "aesthetic" or "style" is, but even that choice should be informed by the more important work of getting to know who you are and what you have to say. If you want to produce authentic work, then what you make should come out of who you are.

So whether you're a photographer, a writer, a singer, or a sculptor, we're rooting for you to do the hard self-work to develop your unique creative voice, because we know how much more evocative your work will be if it comes from this space.

We want your output to be unashamedly influenced by those who have come before you but developed into your own unique method and message.

We want your creative voice to be born of your story and communicate your worldview because, chances are, the things you've seen and choose to share will leave the rest of us feeling less alone.

We want your work to be a reflection of who you are as a singular person and personality because it's the best shot you have at showing the world something we've never seen or heard before.

We need you to do that arduous internal labour and discover who you really are so that you can point those creative skills you've developed at something truly meaningful, for all our sakes.

In short, in the things you make, we need you to be you.

Ego

We had a fairly eccentric art teacher at my high school. He was a short, stocky man who spoke in a sort of rasping, gravelly snarl, so it sounded like he was growling when he talked. It was unnerving at first. Rumour had spread that he was an ex-boxer who had taken a particularly vicious jab to the throat in a bout, which had left him with permanent damage to the vocal cords, but of course, there was no proof of this, and it was almost certainly made up.

He had a temper too.

Most of the time we took his little outbursts as a joke because the things he said sounded so ridiculous. On one occasion, he leant over the boy next to me who was working on a painting and growled, "Westwood!" (The kid's name was "Westmore," but he always got that wrong.) "Too much brown! Brown isn't a colour! It's something you plant your potatoes in! Start again!"

The class giggled until silenced by a glare.

I remember one day, though, when he properly lost it. He was standing up front and stapling together notes for the class when his stapler suddenly decided to cease its dispensing. He snarled at it and opened it up, but it was almost fully loaded. He closed it back up and just tried pressing harder. Still no staples. He then placed it on his desk and began hammering on top of it, tearing holes through the papers, and yelling with each strike, "IT'S-YOUR-ONE-AND-ONLY-JOB!"

At this point, we were all in various states of stifled hysterics and it seemed he suddenly looked up and noticed, which only enraged him further. He lifted the stapler in the air and then began hammering it against his desk, until pieces of dismembered stapler were flying all over the room, and then with a roar he stormed out of the classroom.

There was a shocked silence.

A pause.

Then one of our wittier classmates simply said, "Ah, the artist's temperament," which broke the tension and led to a renewed round of collective laughter.

&

From stories of musicians and their ridiculous green room demands, to actors having tantrums on set when things don't go their way, to the eternal war between the top chefs and food critics, artists are stereotypically known for being fragile creatures with "big egos."

However, this isn't really "Ego." That's a misnomer. These tantrums are often just examples of the bluster that occasionally bursts out of a temporarily unbalanced or insecure Ego.

I think true Ego is an essential guide on our respective journeys as "makers of things," especially if we each intend to use the unique creative voice we've uncovered. Anything novel (acknowledging, of course, that there is nothing truly new under the sun) will divide the room, and for most of us, it's going to take a healthy and balanced Ego to weather the resistance that will almost certainly come our way.

Let's start by defining what we mean by Ego.

In popular language, we often use the word to describe negative traits. "That guy has an Ego on him" is meant to suggest things like arrogance, condescension, conceit, and self-importance. But the fact is that we all have an Ego, every one of us. If we didn't, there would be a big problem.

Sigmund Freud was the one who popularised the use of the word "Ego" back in the early 1900s, but since his original idea, we have changed and watered down its meaning and lost the nuance of his groundbreaking theory. I'm no psychoanalyst, but let me try to break this down in layman's terms.

Freud suggested that our thinking mind is split into three primary modes or drives.

At our most base level is the "Id."

This is what some people call our "lizard brain," which is responsible for our instinctual drives like sex and aggression, the fight-or-flight instinct, and our survival drives for things like food, shelter, and safety. It's that often autonomic part of our mind that is just trying to make sure we keep ourselves alive, procreate to further the species, and eliminate competition for resources.

As you can imagine, the "Id" is invariably selfish and isn't concerned with long-term personal consequences, so it needs tempering. We are all born pure "Id" as babies, but thankfully, we quickly start to develop both an Ego and Superego as we move through childhood.

Now, let's jump to that most outer layer, the "Superego."

This is the part of our minds that is concerned with more than our selfish needs and wants. It's where we store the learned norms of our tribe or society and decide to act for the benefit of all, not just to meet our own selfish desires.

Perhaps you've heard parents at the dinner table telling their children, "In this family, we clear the table after a meal." They're attempting to teach their kids that their seemingly uncontrollable need to run back to their gaming console leaves others to clean up the mess from dinner, and that isn't appropriate. In the bigger picture, parents are trying to show their children that sometimes they need to live for others and delay their own gratification to be able to join the rest of society. They are aiding in the development of their children's social and moral conscience. This is the Superego, and without it, societies couldn't function.

Now, the Ego in Freud's theory was the mediator between the Id and the Superego, between our base instinctual drives and the responsibility we feel toward the rest of humanity.

The Ego negotiates and brings balance.

More importantly for our purposes here, it's in the midst of this internal arbitration that we form our individuality. Our sense of self is forged in the Ego, as it constantly tries to define who this individual is that we inhabit. On the one hand, we are human beings with basic needs that must be met, and on the other hand, we are human beings who need to find a way to fit in with other human beings and balance our needs with theirs. Who you feel you are resides in your Ego, so it has a crucial role to play in the psyche. That makes it neither good nor bad, just necessary.

We spoke in the last chapter about discovering your unique creative voice, and I hope by now it's obvious that your voice will come out of your Ego, which is one of the many reasons we need it.

However, it requires a delicate balance because an uncalibrated Ego can be our undoing. Falling on the one side could mean we can't muster the self-confidence to make things we really believe in, and losing our footing on the other could mean that our inflated sense of self derails us altogether.

&

Let's start with where the Ego is essential.

In my early school years, I was a very shy child. So much so that I would find out much later that my mom would receive letters from concerned teachers saying that they were trying everything to get me involved, but I just refused to engage. Being the shy child I was, there was no more terrifying ordeal for me than the dreaded "English Oral" tests. As a class, we would be asked to prepare a talk roughly 10 minutes long and deliver it to the rest of the class for a grade.

Jerry Seinfeld has a great comedic bit on public speaking in which he says:

A recent survey stated that the average person's greatest fear is having to give a speech in public. Somehow this ranked even higher than death which was third on the list. So, you're telling me that at a funeral, most people would rather be the guy in the coffin than have to stand up and give the eulogy.

As a troubled and introverted kid, I could relate to that sentiment. I would delay preparation in the hopes that the test would miraculously be cancelled, or that the world would end—it really didn't matter which, so long as I didn't have to stand up in front of other people and be judged on how well I spoke.

It was absolutely terrifying.

As the time drew close, though, and it was obvious this was going to happen, I would slink off to the library and hastily paste together a string of facts about some random volcano from an encyclopaedia. I would then walk into class on the dreaded day, sweating, clutching my crumpled notes, willing the ground to open up and swallow me whole.

I was always astounded at how some of the kids managed to breeze through these tests with smiles on their faces. Some even seemed to enjoy it. They didn't just deliver their speeches; they performed them. I wasn't born with the "look-at-me" gene, though, so the experience was always painful and my grades were always low.

My speech usually consisted of me staring down at my tattered piece of paper for the duration, never once glancing up at the rest of the class or the teacher. I shuffled my feet; fiddled nervously with the lectern; and spoke in a rushed, barely discernible mumble.

It was always awful.

So it might come as a surprise that I decided in my late teens and early twenties that I wanted to be a pastor. In all honesty, it came as a surprise to me as well because a big part of the job was to stand up in front of others and speak to large groups of people.

At some point, I had decided that the good I felt I could do working for the church outweighed my own personal discomfort around speaking in public, and I was going to have to get over it.

Unfortunately for me, the seminary felt the same way, and they had a particularly brutal method of helping people face this common fear. We had preaching classes, or "homiletics," as they were called, and if I thought 10-minute English Oral tests in school were a trial, then I was in for a rude awakening.

In homiletics classes, when it was my turn that week, I would have to stand up and deliver a message for 45 minutes. We then took a short break. When we returned, I would then have to sit and listen to the rest of the class tear to pieces what I had just done.

I wasn't allowed to speak; I could only listen to the reviews. No explanations. No justifications. So I had to be quiet as they criticised the construction of my message, the believability of my analogies, the structure of my sentences, the tone of my voice, and the posture of my body. Everything and anything was open to ruthless analysis for what felt like a second never-ending 45 minutes.

I remember coming home after that first homiletics class in which my head had been on the chopping block and feeling completely defeated. I wasn't very good at this and my class, my teacher, and even my friends had let me know it. That day I was trying to work out a way to quit this whole thing gracefully.

My Id was telling me to run and protect myself. Making a fool of myself in front of others like this was just too humiliating.

But my Superego wouldn't let me off the hook. I was still convinced of the good I could do if I kept at it. There was no doubt a painful road ahead if I hung around, but I knew that if I found a way to persist, I could bring hope to people who desperately needed it, and that seemed more important than my own personal comfort, even on a dreadful day like that one.

I needed my Ego. Sitting on my bed, close to tears, I resolved not to leave and to stick it out because the kind of individual I wanted to be would put himself in difficult situations if it would ultimately help others. That seemed like a good human being, and it was my Ego negotiating between the fears of my Id and the ideals of my Superego that helped me to make that choice.

A strange thing happened after that; I started to get pretty good at speaking to groups of people. It took a couple of years of hard work and more humiliating homiletics classes, but it wasn't long before I began to develop a reputation as someone who could take complicated ideas and present them simply to a crowd of people in ways that resonated emotionally. My early jobs in churches required explaining deep spiritual mysteries to distracted teenagers, so this new skill was obviously going to come in handy.

Truth be told, after "burning the ships," so to speak, and committing to sticking it out and getting beyond my fears, I started to enjoy speaking to crowds and began to wonder what more I could do with this skill set.

As I found my courage, I even began to use this creative medium of oratory to challenge the church itself.

I spoke often about our collective hypocrisy toward the poor. We claimed we cared, but we were using all our resources to build fancy buildings with huge sound systems and multimedia screens. There were endless meetings and passionate arguments about the colour of the new carpets but precious little being done for those suffering in our community.

In one particular church, we were prohibited from bringing homeless people from the soup kitchen we ran to Sunday services because "they may mess up the furniture." The last church I worked for even installed spikes outside the front doors so homeless individuals couldn't take shelter under the porch in the rain.

I chose to use the skills I was cultivating in this creative medium to challenge the institution, but it will come as no surprise that talking about these issues made me very unpopular with the establishment.

Something else that made me very unpopular was my choice to speak openly about my own doubts. I felt that if I were going to speak about things we can't see, or hear, or prove, it was essential to acknowledge that we all have doubts. To ignore or deny this was foolish; it would mean that no one would believe us anyway because doubt is human—and an essential ingredient of faith. I shared that I was done taking the Bible literally because I didn't believe it was ever meant to be used that way. I would talk about my own deep doubts about God's level of involvement in a world where bad things constantly happened and how that questioning led to my own dark nights of the soul.

I didn't do it to discourage people—just the opposite. I shared all this because I knew we all experienced the same doubts and fears, and I believed that if we learnt to admit them to each other, we could journey together more openly and perhaps discover a more robust, collective courage to keep going. This was a huge comfort to the younger crowd I was responsible for, but again, a huge problem for the establishment.

Every Monday morning, I would have emails chastising me for the things I had shared the night before from the stage. I was told, "Keep your criticisms of the church to yourself," and, "Good leaders don't share their doubts," but I believed in what I was doing.

It was the negotiations of my Ego that had not only given me the courage to engage in creative oratory in the first place but had now also given me the backbone to say things that I knew would be unpopular and would ultimately lead to my ejection from the church.

I was called every name in the book by those in power. I was arrogant, conceited, proud, opinionated, egotistical, and self-centred. In the minds of many in the establishment, I had a "big ego," but I realised then that Ego is actually an essential ingredient to succeeding in putting your creative voice out there, especially if you are pushing the boundaries.

&

You see, I think any maker of things has to be "self-centred." I understand that "self-centred" is a term traditionally used to describe a bad thing, but let's try and reclaim it. I mean it in the sense that you understand who you are and what you're trying to do, and you back yourself.

One of Aesop's Fables describes why perfectly.

A man and his son were once going with their donkey to market.

As they were walking along by his side a countryman passed them and said, "You fools, what is a donkey for but to ride upon?" So the man put the boy on the donkey, and they went on their way.

But soon they passed a group of men, one of whom said, "See that lazy youngster, he lets his father walk while he rides." So the man ordered his boy to get off and got on himself.

But they hadn't gone far when they passed two women, one of whom said to the other, "Shame on that lazy lout to let his poor little son trudge along." Well, the man didn't know what to do, but at last, he took his boy up before him on the donkey.

By this time they had come to the town, and the passersby began to jeer and point at them. The man stopped and asked what they were scoffing at. The men said, "Aren't you ashamed of yourself for overloading that poor donkey of yours; you and your hulking son?" The man and boy got off and tried to think what to do. They thought and they thought, until at last they cut down a pole, tied the donkey's feet to it, and raised the pole and the donkey to their shoulders.

They went along amid the laughter of all who met them until they came to a bridge, when the donkey, getting one of his feet loose, kicked out and caused the boy to drop his end of the pole. In the struggle, the donkey fell over the bridge, and his forefeet being tied together, he was drowned.

We won't produce anything of worth if we are directed by the crowd because they will all want something different from us. Self-centredness—having an internally grounded belief in what you're trying to do or say with your work—is essential if you're going to make it.

I remember when comedian Ricky Gervais first hosted the Golden Globe Awards back in 2010. He ended up ribbing and roasting celebrities in his usual brutal fashion, and the press was in a rage about his audacity for telling the jokes he did.

It seemed that poking fun at some of the richest and most powerful people in the world was a bridge too far for many. A sector of the public was similarly incensed and went on the attack to reprimand this upstart Brit for denigrating the beloved icons of Hollywood's silver screen.

In the wake of this controversy, Gervais was invited on CNN by Piers Morgan to "explain himself."

I've watched the whole 45-minute interview, which you can still find on YouTube, and at no point does Gervais apologise for the things he said. He reminds Morgan that he is a co-median and the expectation is that a comedian observes and pokes fun at our oddities. "If it isn't true, it isn't funny," which means good jokes necessarily often cut close to the bone.

Whether you think he went too far or not isn't the point; what I found interesting is how he handled the backlash. Watching the interview, I wondered what it must be like to have thousands of people angry at some aspect of your creative output. I mean, here he sits on live TV being pushed to offer an apology with hundreds of thousands of people watching. All he has to do to make this go away is say, "OK, maybe some jokes went a little too far, and I apologise if I hurt anyone's feelings or offended anyone." But instead, he remained calm and unashamed. He offered none of the gen-eralized, waffly contrition that usually quashes these kinds of things.

I found his unassuming confidence impressive. He knew what he wanted to say on that night; in fact, he'd planned every word in fine detail. He also knew some would love it and some would be offended, but as he points out in the interview, "Just because you're offended doesn't mean you're right. Some people are offended by interracial marriage."

He had thought it through, and so the reactions of the media moguls after the fact hadn't shaken him in the least. At one point in the interview, he said, "If you do what you do, for you alone, the way you think it should be done, you're bulletproof."

Now, I know that could just be read as arrogance—and likely was by many, especially by those who were offended—but that wasn't the tone at all. What he was saying was that if you are going to put yourself out there, you have to back yourself. You can't be swayed by everyone's opinion of what you're doing, or you will end up producing work that doesn't affect anyone.

Another comedian, the late Patrice O'Neal, used to say that you don't want everyone at your show to be laughing if you're a progressive comic moving the art form forward. He said that in an audience of 100, he personally "wanted 50 people in hysterics, and 50 people outraged." That's how he knew he was on track with his material, but that takes a healthy Ego and a "self-centred" belief in what you're doing.

I saw it when I started a YouTube channel a few years ago. I had the notion that I would make sure to speak about things vulnerably, in the same way that I did when I spoke in churches. I knew I might get push back from some in the same way that I did with those Monday morning emails, but I also knew it was important.

I was so tired of listening to photographers on YouTube bragging about how busy and wealthy and popular they were, and how business was just booming for them. I remember how depressing it was listening to this stuff when I was getting started in the field because everyone just seemed to be so successful. What was I doing wrong?

It took me ages to realise most of them had been lying, or "inflating the truth" to market themselves.

So I made the choice to be honest about both the ups and downs of the creative journey when I shared anything online, and the backlash came immediately.

It seems that vulnerability infuriates a particular brand of mostly men who believe that portraying strength and being loud is good marketing. This group is usually trying to convince us, and themselves, that life has been one long run of "win" after "win," but for most of us, our journeys are a messy struggle with no guarantees. It certainly has been for me, but sharing that openly made some people very angry. It's not how the game is played.

In the minds of a few vocal commenters, I was "killing people's dreams" by suggesting that there are no guarantees, no matter how hard they work, but I know that when I heard honest people sharing their own challenges along the way, it gave me great comfort as someone following in their wake. In those rare moments, I found myself on the other end of the equation, receiving comfort from someone else's vulnerability in the same way I had been able to give comfort to confused teens in the church through my own vulnerability. Their openness and honesty rescued me from beating myself up when things didn't work out, helping me recalibrate my expectations, which ultimately kept me going. My goal online was always to give that gift to others.

When that backlash started to roll in, it again took conviction in what I was doing to keep going. I still get called pretentious, egotistical, and arrogant for refusing to change course when people decry some aspect of what I'm doing, but you can't please everyone, and you may always be seen in a negative light by those who disagree with you. There's nothing you can do about that.

This is also apparent in my street photography. I get flack from other street photographers who say it isn't valid "street photography" because the work I produce isn't reportage, but more stylised. I'm OK with that. I'm following in the footsteps of photographers whose work I love, like Ray Metzker, Trent Parke, and Fan Ho, who also took more abstract images and played with light, shadow, and shape. Honestly, I don't care what label you give the images I take.

At the end of the day, they are the images I want to see more of, and so I make them assuming there may be others out there who also want to see this sort of work, and I'm going to keep doing it whether it fits into a particular box or not.

That can sound arrogant, but I think that a healthy "self-centredness" is essential if you are going to blaze your own trail. It's the only way to ensure that your creative endeavours have focus, because if you fall into the trap of trying to please everyone and produce for the widest possible audience, you'll end up reaching no one effectively.

I used to think that the worst thing that could happen would be that my work was rejected, but I've since realised that it's not. The worst thing that could happen would be that I tried to please everyone around me and ended up putting out ineffectual, middle-of-the-road blandness for fear of offending anyone. That sort of work is so easy to ignore, and if that happened, I would have no one to blame but myself.

We can take the risk of "yelling" something we believe confidently with the message or the method of our creative output, or we can "whisper" something mediocre softly in a corner for fear of being heard and shunned. I know which I would prefer to do, and that requires a healthy Ego because it will serve to constantly remind me of who I am and what I want to say. It will help me conjure up the courage to back myself in the face of the inevitable criticism that will come.

&

You can see the danger straight away, though, can't you? It's a very short step away from being that "egotist" who won't listen, who has an inflated opinion of themselves and what they do, and who doesn't care about anyone but themselves. It's a fine balance to be struck.

I've lost that balance before, many times.

I told you that after a couple of years I was not only pretty adept at speaking in public but I also began to get a name for it. On occasion I found myself speaking to crowds of a couple of thousand people, and listening to the long line of admirers giving me compliments afterwards. It was a little difficult to keep my head from inflating. The positive attention I was getting for the creative skill I had built for myself was intoxicating. If I'm very honest with you, and I want to be, I might have been the picture of self-deprecating humility on the outside, but I had become pretty ugly and arrogant about it on the inside.

Ego can get in the way if we don't keep it in check.

We can be taken off track and tempted to chase adulation.

We can be so self-assured that we stop listening to how our work lands with others.

We can become defensive in the face of reasonable feedback.

We can use our creative talents to grandstand for ourselves rather than communicate with others.

We all have a potential "show off" in us waiting to be let off the leash, but once he's off, it's difficult to get him back under control.

One of my favourite speakers and authors is a Franciscan friar by the name of Richard Rohr, and I've heard him define our Ego's worst impulses like this: "The human Ego wants two things; it wants to be separate and superior." When left to its own devices, our Ego can take us to dark places as it attempts to play this game.

Sexism is allowing ourselves to think we are "separate and superior" to others because of our gender.

Racism is allowing ourselves to think we are "separate and superior" to others because of the colour of our skin.

Nationalism is allowing ourselves to think we are "separate and superior" to others because of the chance event of our birth within a set of geographical borders.

So what about artists?

Well, when we lose balance, our Ego can tip over from giving us the courage and self-assurance we need to make the things we do to whispering in our ear that our talent makes us different from others—special, perhaps even fundamentally better. We have to get good at identifying when we are losing this delicate balance because it will poison the well of our creativity if left unchecked.

Something strange happened when I lost this balance for myself. I can pinpoint the year I started to get cocky about my newfound confidence around speaking in public, and it was the same year that I actually began to get worse. I would showboat more than necessary, my stories got longer and more self-indulgent, and I think I began to take on a condescending tone. The biggest problem was that I wasn't the first to pick it up; everyone else was, and this will often be the case.

I think people can tell when something comes from a place of humility and vulnerability, and when it comes from someone who believes they are better than you, and the latter is infinitely less attractive and will completely undermine the message.

It took a few months of internal suspicion about how off-course I was, and one particularly pointed review (which I will get to later in this book) to get honest with myself about the ugly imbalance that had crept in. I course-corrected hard, but it took a good year for people to trust that the arrogant "me" had been sent packing for good.

Richard Rohr speaks to large crowds of people around the world and has been very honest about his own struggles with Ego. I've even heard him say that he prays for "one good humiliation every day" just to keep him grounded and remind him of his frail humanity. He does it so that when the praise and adulation comes, he doesn't believe the lie that he is any better than you or I.

The ancient Romans knew this.

When a general won a great military campaign, he could be granted the honour of a triumph, which was a giant parade of troops, treasures, and captured slaves through the streets of Rome. The procession would be headed up by the general himself, bedecked in finery on a gilded chariot, with throngs of adoring citizens lining the streets, cheering on his courage and great deeds.

But behind the general on his chariot stood a slave who held a laurel wreath—the symbol for victory—above his head. This slave had a very specific job to do. He was required to constantly whisper into the general's ear, "You are only a man." "You are only a man." The ancient Romans knew well the danger of tyrannical kings, and they were intent on reminding generals that, whilst their deeds deserved praise, they were still just another citizen, and their work was done in service of the people, not themselves.

As "makers of things," when the adulation comes in, we need to be our own "whispering voice" to bring balance by constantly reminding ourselves that we're only human. No matter how great a painter, singer, writer, or filmmaker you are, you are fundamentally no better than anyone else, and this gift you have to give was meant to elevate others, not yourself.

The Ego is our trickster guide.

On the one hand, Ego will guide you to make the work you believe in, give you the grit to back yourself, and imbue you with the courage to continue on, even in the face of criticism and doubt.

On the other hand, it's a common phenomenon that many artists make their best work before they become well-known. For some, once they gain that notoriety, they never manage to reach those pre-fame heights in their work again.

"Their first album was their best."

"Her early paintings were some of my favourites."

"After the early struggle, his work just became boring and derivative."

I wonder if part of the reason is that they allowed the worst impulses of their Egos to steal their focus. I can't be sure, but it does remind me never to let self-importance distract me from making beautiful things.

The dance of the Ego is learning, on the one hand, to ward off the possibility that it turns us into someone we don't like and whose work has nothing to say, and on the other hand, it's using our Ego as the fuel and confidence we need to keep going and to give us a direction for the things that we make.

Control

Five years ago now, I took myself on a solo retreat to Snowdonia in Wales.

At the time, work had been getting a little overwhelming. This was back when I was photographing a seemingly never-ending line of products every day, and picking up my camera had gone from being exciting to disheartening; I needed a break. So I took my own advice and chose to get away to this picturesque mountainous region for a few days, in the hope that making space and breathing in might lead to some much-needed in-spiration.

Rather than just taking the time off, I decided to give myself two tasks.

First, I wanted to try my hand at landscape photography. It's not a form of photography I had any experience in at that point, but I reasoned that attempting something brand-new and throwing myself into the deep end could only be invigorating and provide a necessary counterpoint to the predictable sort of photography I did for my day job.

Second, I decided to film it. I would create a video diary of the things I learned on the trip, both about photography and about myself. Honestly, at the time I didn't have any intention of sharing it; I just knew I would be on my own for four days, and even when I take breaks, I like to give my hands something creative to do.

I had booked a small cabin by a river in the Ogwen Valley and arrived amid less-than-ideal conditions. It was late April and spring was struggling to break. The skies were lead grey and snow flurries were blowing through the valleys, so on the first night, I opted to head to my warm bed early and read a book.

I was up early the next morning, hopeful that the light would be better, but it wasn't. In fact, for the next three days, the weather was typically Welsh and I managed to take only a handful of mediocre photographs as I explored the valleys.

Filming was even less successful, but I plucked up the necessary courage to record two short pieces to camera, describing the techniques I was using to get particular shots. The rest of the time, I was huddled in my car with the heater on, driving around and listening to podcasts, or parked and reading a book in front of a promising vista, praying for the light to break through.

On the last morning, I had very little to show for my time there, but I didn't mind because the break had been a good one. Trips like this aren't about being productive; they are about creating that generative space we spoke about earlier. All that time sitting and processing had been refreshing, and trying out landscape photography had stretched me creatively, which felt good too.

On the final morning, as I sat on the wooden deck overlooking the river with a cup of coffee in hand I started to inventory the footage I had collected. On top of those two clips I had recorded to camera, I had also shot some B roll of the valleys and even put my new drone up a couple of times to get sweeping shots of the lakes and mountains.

I took out my notebook and sketched out a rough edit for the footage, and it immediately became clear that there wasn't nearly enough material to create a meaningful film. So, just as an exercise, I began to write a three-part monologue—an intro, middle, and outro—that would piece everything together, to see if I could have made a video if I had planned things a little better.

It took half an hour or so, and I looked at the page and felt a little disappointed in myself for not sketching things out sooner because it seemed as if I could have pulled something together with a bit more time and planning. I told myself again that this was meant to be a break, and I wasn't about to embark on a guilt trip.

I closed my notebook and set it aside.

It was too late to do anything about it anyway.

I went back to sipping my coffee.

Or was it?

In a very uncharacteristic moment for me, I decided to get up and film those pieces I had just scripted, even though I knew they would be rushed and messy. Being short on time, I couldn't drive around to multiple locations to film those segments, so I walked to three different spots, all no more than 100 meters from my little cabin. I even switched my jackets and sweaters for each location to make it seem as if I'd filmed on three different days, and despite my abiding discomfort at sitting and talking to a camera, I recorded those three monologues.

Then I packed up hastily to make the check out time, got in the car, and started making my way back to London. Driving back, I was still pretty sure I would never show anyone this video. I knew the footage was weak, I knew the pieces to camera were hurried and unpolished, and I was embarrassed about the landscape images because they were over-edited and poorly composed, showing my lack of experience in this area. Nothing about what I had produced was "good work" in my mind, but once again I reminded my inner drill sergeant that it didn't matter. I was returning home refreshed, and that's why I went in the first place.

It took me a couple of weeks to get around to editing that footage. It didn't seem important because it was just for me, but on a free Saturday, I decided to play around with the edit and see if I could pull something together. However, as things took shape on the timeline, I began to warm to it. I even started to consider posting it to my Facebook page for friends to see because it made for a nice little story, and they wouldn't judge me too harshly for the shoddy footage and images.

The edit came together very fast. It was a 16-minute video in total, complete by that afternoon—and I've learned to pay attention to when things flow easily because it's often a sign that you're on the right track. Watching it back, all the flaws were still staring me in the face and I winced at various points, but there was something else about it. It was honest.

I was still torn as to what to do with it, if anything, so I showed it to a couple of close friends and asked what they thought. When they saw it, they were enthusiastic and encouraged me to post it to the YouTube channel I had abandoned a while ago. That seemed a very risky prospect. The Internet is full of vicious trolls who would love to lambaste my amateurish fumblings at landscape photography, and I really didn't feel like exposing myself to that.

Still, this little film had Logos. Technically, it was a bit of a mess, but it was capital "T" True. I was honest about burning out at work and open about being out of my depth with landscape photography, and that vulnerability and the open attempt at something new to get out of a creative rut made for a good story. It took some self-talk and Ego negotiation to give me the courage to believe in the good parts enough to even consider my friends' advice, but eventually, even though I still felt very unsure, I uploaded the file to YouTube and clicked the button to post it live.

I deliberately left the house after that and went out to catch a movie because I didn't want to worry about who was watching it, or have to read any of the mean comments that would doubtless flood in. However, when I returned home hours later and gathered the courage to take a peek, I was completely taken aback by the overwhelmingly warm response to it. I found it really moving that most people seemed to graciously ignore the filming errors and the inept landscape photography and embraced the message.

For those of you who encountered me on YouTube before you picked up this book, you'll likely know that this one video set the tone for the channel I run today. Now you also know the story behind it and how close that little film was to never being made, and consequently, how close that channel was to never getting off the ground.

For those who are reading this as their first interaction with me, it's the films I've made on that channel in the last five years that have built toward writing this book. So even the chain of events leading to you sitting here and reading these words began with a burnt-out photographer finding the courage to show the world a little video he had made, which he really wasn't sure about at all.

You see, I'm a perfectionist. It's one of the biggest obstacles holding me back from making and then sharing the things I make.

There is a misconception that perfectionists are lucky because they have some sort of finely tuned, internal quality control that means that everything they put out is pure gold. I had someone say to me once, "I wish I was a perfectionist." If you knew what it really is, you wouldn't wish it on your worst enemy. The reality is that perfectionism is often crippling because it's based in fear. Specifically, perfectionists are afraid to put anything out into the world that they can't guarantee will be universally hailed as "great work."

The obvious problem is that no one can guarantee that. Ever. Deep down the perfectionist knows that too, and the unfortunate result is that they never want to put out anything at all because they can't guarantee the outcome, so many are constantly producing good work that they then hide from everyone else out of fear.

You'll know when you've stepped into a perfectionist's creative workspace because it will be full of really good pieces of work that are in the process of being hidden, discarded, or destroyed. You might have caught yourself at a friend's house at some point looking at drawings they've done or hearing music they've written and found yourself perplexed as to why they aren't sharing it with the rest of the world. Maybe you told them how good their work was and tried to convince them to share it with the rest of us. Maybe they even promised you they would think about it, but the way they gathered up the work to hide it from prying eyes told you it would never see the light of day.

In these cases, you're likely dealing with a tormented perfectionist. If they can't guarantee everyone will think their work is brilliant, if they have any doubts at all, their work will be hidden away on a dark top shelf or be consigned to the rubbish bin.

That's unfortunate for two reasons.

First, and most obviously, it's unfortunate for us. Just because it's not the best piece of work ever made doesn't mean it isn't capable of bringing the rest of us great joy or comfort, but the perfectionist's fear will keep us from ever receiving that.

Second, it's unfortunate for the perfectionist. The best way to learn and grow as "makers of things" is to show people what we've made and to see what response we get to our work. That feedback loop helps us assess how our work is landing with others and gives us useful information that assists us in making course corrections going forward. Perfectionists deny themselves that and often stall their own development.

Even if you don't specifically identify as a perfectionist, I think every artist at some point struggles with the fear of releasing their work into the world. Do any of the following statements sound familiar?

"I just have too many ideas. I don't know where to start."

"I really need conditions to be perfect to be able to create."

"I'd love to show people what I'm doing, but I just don't think anyone else will get it."

"I know I've been working on this piece for ages, but it's still not right, so no one can see it."

These might just be rationales we've built to disguise our fears around finishing and sharing what we make.

Five years ago on that retreat, I had started to get honest with myself about this crippling internal paralysis and my own well-worn excuses, and that's why posting that video online that day was such a victory for a recovering perfectionist.

I am by no means cured, and I still battle perfectionism daily, but let me share something with you that has at least given me a mental tool to put those fears in context when they inevitably surface. Again, you may not suffer this level of paralysis, nor identify as a "perfectionist" specifically, but we all have fears about sharing our work with others, and I think this simple principle can be very helpful.

In my case, I learnt this truth from reading about the Stoic philosophers, but I want to acknowledge before diving into this idea that Buddhism, Taoism, some of Jesus' teachings, 12-step programs, and I'm sure many other traditions echo much the same thing. This isn't a new idea, and in fact, the wisest human beings all over the globe and throughout history have intuited this freeing concept.

From Epictetus:

"The chief task in life is simply this: to identify and separate matters so that I can say clearly to myself which are matters not under my control, and which have to do with the choices I actually control."

The idea is simple: we have to learn to stop trying to control things that are beyond our control, and we start by learning where our agency begins and ends.

There are obviously some things you can control but not as many as you might assume in the grand scheme of things. You can control your own words and actions, but that's about it. You can't control anything external to you, and I think the problems we get ourselves into and the anxieties we create for ourselves are often due to our misunderstanding how far our command extends. In reality, when we are talking about total control, it's very limited.

Let me use myself as an example. As a photographer, what can I control?

I can teach myself aggressively. I can read books and look at the work of great photographers to give myself a broad understanding of this medium I am engaged in. I can take a lot of photographs because I'm only going to learn by "doing," making mistakes, learning from them, and "doing" again.

I can put money aside, if I have it, to purchase the equipment I need. I can practice long and hard until using my camera, lenses, and lights is second nature. I can fine-tune my post-processing techniques so that they subtly add quality to my work instead of distracting from it.

If I intend to work as a photographer, I can put myself out there. I can make the effort to market myself to try and bring in work. I can attempt to build a following around what I do on social media platforms to create a name for myself. I can build relationships with others in the industry, which will hopefully lead to connections that could prove useful down the line. I can ask for meetings with people who might want to hire me for the sort of photography I do. I can do unpaid personal projects that could attract the attention of the right people in the long run.

I can take personal responsibility for defining a style by making a thousand tiny choices "for" and "against" the details in my work until something coherent emerges. I can work hard to get to know myself and decide what I want to say with my work. I can teach myself how to respond better to setbacks, and I can put goals in place to make sure I stay on track with the course I have set for myself. I can fight to stay self-aware about how good I am today and how far I still have to go in order to stay sober and motivated for the long road ahead.

All these things are within my power to attempt as I take personal responsibility for my words and actions in pursuing my growth as a photographer. That may sound like a long list, but none of these guarantees me "success," however I choose to define that.

That's because everything else is outside of my control.

Before we get back to photography specifically, let's just admit that the list of things we can't control as individual human beings is infinite: the weather, sports results, bureaucracy, health, global economies, the past, the present, and the winds of change. How much untold strife and pain do we cause ourselves because we keep banging our heads against brick walls trying to control things we can't?

So much of our personal anxiety in the modern world is wrapped up in our frustration around not being able to Order the Chaos, and that lack of self-awareness about our limits can surface the worst in us. Just watch someone yell at a station attendant in furious anger about a late train. It doesn't get them anywhere any faster because it's not in their control—or the station attendant's control for that matter—and that behaviour simply ruins everyone's day.

Relationships are ruined when we try to manipulate our partner's actions instead of accepting that the only things in our power are communicating our own needs, being a good partner ourselves, and deciding whether to stay or go. We can offer the best partner possible to our respective others but still have our relationships dissolve because we control only our half of the whole.

People all over the world are feeling like failures for not getting that last job promotion, when the only thing that was ever in their power was to do the best job they could and to decide whether to stay or go. Success in exchange for diligence was never honestly promised to anyone. We can do the very best job we can, but we may never rise through the ranks because we only control our actions, not our bosses' decisions.

Similarly, when it comes to the things we make, we can do the very best work we're capable of, but we can never control how it's received by the rest of the world. In my own experience, even prediction is impossible. The reason we can't guarantee the response we'll get when we share what we've made is that we are bouncing it off other people with their own agency, tastes, hang-ups, and choices. The things we share are only half of the equation, so no matter how deliberate we are about the things we make, once released our work will always generate a soup of responses and interpretations beyond our control.

Here's the tough truth: even if I work tirelessly at my relationships, my jobs, or my creative pursuits, there is no guarantee that my efforts will produce the outcomes I want or believe I deserve. I am human and limited in my powers. I know this will be unpopular with some, not least because in Western culture particularly, the most fundamental capitalists amongst us tell anyone who will listen that "hard work always equals success" in whatever you attempt, but we know from experience that's not true. If you're like me, you can count many times in your life when you wanted something badly and you worked for it with everything you had, but it still didn't pan out.

That's life, and admitting it to ourselves might just be the key to shedding some guilt and enjoying life more. For me, it's certainly been the key in beginning to overcome my fears about sharing the things I make.

Let's go back to that example of my photography.

I have worked really hard to build a varied set of photography skills. I'm sure I've crossed the fabled 10,000-hour mark at this point, and even though I can still see a long road of development ahead, I know I am no slouch as a photographer.

That said, I still receive negative responses to my work daily. I have to field unkind comments from people who are trying to poke holes in the things I share. I'm not taken seriously by many of my peers, not least because in the minds of many, if you're also a filmmaker on a platform like YouTube, then that somehow discredits you as a serious photographer.

When it comes to supporting myself financially, I have struggled for over a decade to secure a consistent flow of photography work and failed for many seasons to keep my head above water, sometimes having to go back to waiting tables to pay the rent. I had assumed that once I reached a certain level of proficiency and produced a portfolio that displayed what I was capable of, the floodgates would open, my calendar would fill up, and so would my bank account.

In my own personal work, I thought that after building a modest following I would be able to post my images for sale on my website as large signed prints and survive, or even thrive, on the revenue. I have friends who have done the same and they make a good living that way, but I certainly haven't. In my case, it just hasn't worked out like that.

So does all this "failure" mean I'm a bad photographer and that I should just give up?

Well, this is the problem, isn't it? If you believe the lie that hard work automatically equals success and then success doesn't come, then you have to conclude it must be your fault for not working hard enough, and with that false conclusion comes a lot of guilt.

Even if I reject that notion and feel I have actually worked as hard as I was able and things still haven't worked out the way I hoped, then maybe it's even worse? Maybe I have no innate talent in the first place, and I'm fooling myself.

These feelings of guilt and failure, and this lie we tell ourselves about being able to control the results and responses to our work, are why a lot of us would just rather make the things we like and hide them away from the world than deal with the inevitable self-flagellation.

However, let me be clear: I don't feel like a failure at all. I'm very proud of the journey I've been on and how much I've been able to grow my skills and hone my vision. I don't take the fact that I get negative feedback or struggle for photography work as a sign that I am being lazy, or that I'm a talentless failure. When I allow myself a little perspective and grant myself a little kindness, I know that almost every photographer gets negative comments and struggles for work, and most of us fail outright to realise our lofty dreams.

&

Life isn't fair, and the minute we get that through our heads and stop trying to control things we can't, we can shed the fear and guilt that kills our motivation.

Let me give you one more from the Stoics, this time from Seneca:

"The greatest obstacle to living is expectancy, which hangs upon tomorrow and loses today. You are arranging what is in Fortune's control and abandoning what lies in yours."

I hope this Truth frees you as it did me. If you've been dangling the "promise of guaranteed success" in front of yourself as motivation, I hope you can find a way to replace it with "pride in your work" as the reason to keep going and doing the very best you can. The way I think about it is, as long as I can honestly say that I have been diligent with everything that is in my power, then I can stop making myself feel guilty for everything outside of it because those things were never in my control in the first place.

That's why I think learning this lesson about the limits of your control can break the cycle of perfectionism. If, with self-awareness and honesty, I can say to myself that I've done my best today, and then admit that the results and responses to this painting, or poem, or piece of prose are not in my power, I may find the courage to release it into the world. I can remind myself that despite the messy mix of responses my work will inevitably generate, it could also communicate Logos to someone, or it could serve as another artist's in-breath. My act of making could do some real good if I found the pluck to share it.

"Success" isn't your responsibility, but doing the very best job you can is. I hope that simple truth brings you the comfort it does me.

One big criticism of the Stoic philosophers from those who don't really understand what they're saying is, "If you teach yourself not to care about the results, how do you stay ambitious, motivated, and hungry in your work?"

I think the answer is simple—by focussing on the only thing that was ever in your hands in the first place: doing the very best work you can for the sheer joy of it. If fame and fortune are your drivers, then your motivation will dip and rise with the successes and failures you can't control. However, if your motivation lies in the pride you take in your work and the personal responsibility you take for your development, then it has a chance of staying consistent because it's a self-contained system.

I didn't pick up a camera to get famous or rich; I did it because I loved the act and art of making images. I'll admit that I have to remind myself of that regularly, but every time I internally confirm that my joy truly comes from the "making" itself, things become simple once more and I'm motivated to get out the door with my camera in hand.

What do you make? Do you paint? Do you write? Do you dance? Do you remember the early excitement around creating something new before it got so complicated? Do you remember a time before the expectations of success and "good reviews" around your work began to mount? That's what we constantly have to try and recapture in our work. We have to fight the temptation to mentally feed our hunger for things outside our power and instead feed our love of the art form we've chosen because it's all that will sustain us in the long run.

I noticed that when I learned this lesson about control on a broad level, it also started to filter through on a granular level.

As a photographer, I can be too inflexible. Fear makes me stick to more rigid compositions or traditional lighting setups that I know will give my photo a better chance of being seen as a "successful" image by others and help me avoid criticism.

I use a pocket-sized, point-and-shoot camera when I'm out taking photos on the street. It's a great little camera because of its small size and nondescript appearance, so I'm less likely to "bruise the scene" as Joel Meyerowitz would say. However, I still tend to use it like a traditional camera, composing rigid shots and even standing still as if I had a tripod out. This camera begs to be used "fast and loose" but fear of "getting it right" stiffens me up to shoot more traditionally.

The other day I was out taking photos, lining up a shot across the road, when I noticed someone approaching out of the corner of my eye on my side of the street. He was wearing a blue suit, which I realised would contrast nicely against the rusted red railings I was standing next to. There was no time to compose anything, and I knew my shutter speed was set too slow so the motion would be blurred, but I flicked the camera up and instinctively took the shot. The resulting image was certainly more abstract than the shots I usually take, but I really liked it.

It suddenly occurred to me that I was stuck in a rut of my own making and that I have a very particular way of taking images. This image, shot instinctually, reminded me of the importance of experimentation. If we want to produce work that is full of life, which breaks the rules and makes us think, then we also need to overcome that clutching need to control everything. Sticking to the rules too closely and holding things too tightly can choke the life from our creativity, but giving ourselves permission to play loosely with our art form will unlock new avenues of expression.

One "accidental" photograph had served to remind me that the best way to develop ourselves is to experiment and play, which takes courage if people are watching because we have to risk that they won't get it. When I shared that particular photograph online, a series of bemused comments followed, telling me that I'd "lost it." This sort of response doesn't matter, though, because in my most sane and sober moments, I know that if I only make work that has a high probability of pleasing the crowd, then rigidity and repetition will creep in and I'll stagnate.

We will only be happy and mentally healthy "makers of things" if we admit to ourselves that we control only the work we produce and our own development as artists. Felt anxiety around the responses to our work is not going to move the needle even a millimetre, and in my experience desperately trying to control things you can't just winds up hurting people, especially yourself. You won't win. It's when we let go of trying to control the responses or to control our work too tightly that we can return to the simple joy of making, sharing, and growing as an artist, which, again, takes a healthy and balanced Ego.

So maybe it's time to let yourself off the hook. Admit to yourself where your influence begins and ends, and learn to release the rest. It's time to transfer that mental energy from expectations around the results, to just pushing yourself to do your best and being the most conscientious, hard-working artist you can. That way, when all is said and done, if you haven't "succeeded" in the way you hoped, you'll know it wasn't because you neglected the things you could control, and hopefully, you can graciously accept that it was due to things that were never in your hands in the first place—and that's OK.

&

I used to regularly attend a live music show at The World's End pub in Finsbury Park. It ran on Sunday nights and was a small affair, weekly featuring a different lineup of three singer-songwriters who each performed five original songs they had written. It became a tradition that the pub would bring up trays of leftover roast potatoes, gravy, and Yorkshire puddings from lunch, and we could feast, free of charge whilst enjoying the music. Our host, Kal, a talented musician in her own right, would begin the evening by reminding us of the one rule, which we were expected to shout with her in unison at the evening's opening: "While the acts are playing, SHUT THE F#*! UP!"

What impressed me every night I attended was the stratospheric quality of the talent on that stage, but with the exception of Ed Sheeran, you probably won't have heard of any of the incredible musicians who played those intimate "We Love Sundays" shows.

Week after week, I watched a parade of exceptional artists perform their hearts out and felt the injustice in seeing these talented individuals playing such incredible music to a small room of 40 patrons, all stuffing our faces and wiping gravy from our chins. As respectful and grateful as we were to be there, and as rapturous as our applause was, I felt as if they should be performing for stadiums of adoring fans and having their music played across the globe on radio stations.

But as we've firmly established, the world isn't a fair place, and it doesn't automatically reward talent and hard work with our neat definitions of success. However, so many of those artists seemed to have come to terms with this fact already. They didn't seem to care about the crowd size, and they rarely came across as feeling entitled to more than they had. They played for the sheer love of it, and I believe they gave their performance the same energy and effort as they would have if performing for 50,000 screaming fans and being paid exorbitant sums of money. They took pride in their work. I have no doubt they had the same internal battles you and I do, but they still chose to generously share their gift with the world, and that left a big impression on me.

I hope likewise that you find the courage to share what you're making with the rest of us. I can't promise you it will make you rich. I can't say whether you will achieve the level of success you dream of. I certainly can't guarantee that people will say only nice things about it, but if you can find it within you to show us that thing you've been working on, I know there is a chance it could benefit someone somewhere.

There is this great story about Michelangelo and his work of sculpture called *The Deposition*. It depicts Jesus being lowered from the cross by three figures, most likely the Virgin Mary, Mary Magdalene, and Nicodemus. Michelangelo had been working on it for eight years when, one night in 1555, he attempted to destroy the piece in a fit of rage.

Scholars disagree about the reasons why. Some say the marble wasn't behaving the way he wanted it to, and he lost his temper with it. Some say he had used himself as a model for the figure of Nicodemus, and he was worried it could betray his sympathies for Luther and the Reformation movement, which could have landed him in a lot of hot water. Some say the artist suddenly worried that Christ's left leg hanging lifeless over the Virgin Mary's lap might convey too much eroticism and be misconstrued, so it had to come off, as well as other limbs and appendages. Whatever the reason, he was done with this piece.

However, he was halted in his destructive actions, and the sculpture was saved from annihilation and restored by another artist named Calcagni, who reattached Mary Magdalene's limbs, the Virgin's fingers, and Christ's arms; and then did his best to complete the work. It lives today in the Museo dell'Opera del Duomo and brings joy and awe to many who come to see it, especially the devout, despite its obvious flaws, including Christ's still-absent left leg.

None of us is above these fears and this desire to control outcomes. On this occasion, Michelangelo himself seems to have lost a battle with his own concerns over how his work would be viewed and, were it not for the interventions of others, this piece may now be nothing more than a nondescript pile of rubble.

It's time to own your fears and release control. You don't have to achieve perfection before you let the rest of us enjoy what you made. As Sheryl Sandberg famously said, "Done is better than perfect." She's right of course, especially if "perfect" means we never get to see your work but "done" means it's released into the world where it at least has the potential to bring the rest of us comfort and joy.

Attention

My dad left home when I was four years old.

I obviously don't remember that time well because I was just too young. The vague memories I have, which have been confirmed by many family members since, are that my dad was my hero at that age. The highlight of my day was when he would come home after work and take me out into the garden to kick a ball around or throw me into the air until his arms ached.

Sadly, he left our family for another woman, and my mom suddenly had some important decisions to make. She was now a single mother to my six-month-old brother and me, and she realised she needed as much help as she could get. So, as much as we loved Africa, she packed us up and moved us from our home in Zimbabwe back to the UK to be closer to extended family.

From all accounts, I changed overnight. I went from being a fairly confident and talkative child to the shy, quiet, and unsure little boy who would soon be terrified of English Oral exams. The breakup of our nuclear family and the sudden absence of my dad served to shake my fledgling develop-ment, and at the time it felt safer to retreat inward. It's a story that has been repeated millions of times, with count-less children all over the world, and those who have been through the breakup of a family at a young age themselves will know how rudderless it leaves you feeling. My mom did her best, I'm sure, to try and bring up two small children on her own, all the while attempting to deal with her own grief around losing the love of her life. But despite all her efforts, the next few years were pretty rough and lonely.

About four years later, we moved back to Africa, this time settling in Botswana. There my mom met a man, got pregnant, and remarried. I remember being so excited that I would be getting a dad. Children are often (thankfully) kept out of their parents' dating lives, so I hadn't spent much time with this man yet, but I assumed all that would change once things were official. I would suddenly have access to him, and that father-shaped hole in my little-boy soul would be filled.

It wasn't to be.

Shortly after they were married, I remember calling him "Dad" for the first time. I tried to make it sound casual and normal, even though it felt like anything but. On the inside I was nervous with anticipation, hoping that this would be the start of something good and new. So I was crushed, as you can imagine, when his response was to cut me short and tell me, "I'm not your father, Sean. When your sister is born in a few weeks, I will be her father, but I'm not yours."

I don't think he was a bad man; he just had no idea how to deal with children, and as much as he loved my mom, he wasn't interested in a package deal where he had to take on someone else's kids as his own. Of course, I can understand all that as an adult, but as a child that rejection, coupled with the isolation that would come when my half-sister took centre stage, only caused me to retreat ever deeper into myself.

One day, on a trip back to the UK to visit family, we went down to the coast to spend a day in a little seaside town. We walked around for a few hours looking at the quaint shops; then when our legs got tired, we got some greasy, vinegary hot chips wrapped in newspaper from a local "chippy" and went to sit near the harbour to watch the boats come in.

I had recently been given a camera for my birthday. It was one of those plastic point-and-shoot film cameras that made that distinctive "zip-zip" sound when you wound on the film. I loved that little camera. Not only had I quickly realised that I really enjoyed taking photographs, but it also did double duty as a prop that I used as a shy child when I felt I needed some space. If I looked as if I were taking photographs, adults wouldn't feel the need to ask me what I was doing all the time because a quick glance would give them their answer, and they would leave me in peace.

Those of you who have visited the Devonshire coast will be familiar with the seagulls: a particular airborne nuisance who will appear in droves the minute hot chips are unwrapped from their papery packaging. This occasion was no different, and as we ate, an ominous, feathered cloud formed overhead. As we hurriedly scarfed down our food and fought off the flying menace, a seagull landed on the railing in front of me, and I saw an opportunity for a photograph. I wrapped up my chips, picked up my camera, and began stalking forward. He didn't move. Maybe he thought I was bringing him a treat. Perhaps his familiarity with humans had rendered him unconcerned by my proximity, but for whatever reason he let me get very close to him. When I was no more than a meter away, he finally cocked his head and flinched as if to fly off. I froze, realising this was as close as he would allow me. I slowly raised my camera and took the photograph.

A week or two later, my mom had the film developed and I remember sitting at the kitchen table leafing through the prints. When we got to that shot of the seagull, my mom took the photograph from my hand to look at it closer and said, "That's a good picture. Maybe you'll be a photographer."

In her mind, it may have been a throwaway comment, but in my mind, I felt a rush of warm affirmation and my chest swelled with pride. It was like oxygen to an unsure young boy who felt directionless and doubtful of his own worth. I don't want to make it sound as if my mom wasn't supportive in general because she definitely was, and I couldn't tell you why that one comment made such an impression on me, only that it did. That single compliment took root deep down, and it was the first day I can clearly remember feeling the exhilaration of being praised, validated, and affirmed because of something I had made, and that feeling was addictive.

I've had to ask myself many times since that day, "Have I just been creating to get people to like me?" It would be many years before I came back around and landed on photography as a career path, but in those intervening years, had I started bands because I liked screaming crowds? Did I speak in public because I liked the rapt attention of an audience? Did I make little films because the best of them elicited an emotional response from viewers and accompanying praise for having stirred them? Did I eventually come back to taking photographs because people gave me compliments about them, starting with my mom decades ago? How much of my creativity was driven by the fact that deep down I have always had to contend with the rootless little boy inside who is endlessly looking for affirmation and his place in this world?

We all have that inner child in us looking for approval. From our earliest days when our parents took those drawings we did and thought them worthy of the vaunting heights of the fridge door, we have been chasing that affirmation from our fellow human beings. Approval feels good, and it should, which makes it a powerful motivator. It gives us a sense of belonging, worth, value, and connection to others. The things we make can deliver us that sort of feedback from others, and it's intoxicating. However, we have to remain vigilant and be honest with ourselves when our need for approval becomes unhealthy and tips over from a normal desire for acceptance to the sort of neediness that can lead us astray.

Now, I'm not for a minute suggesting that all creation comes from a place of neediness. We all rightly feel that our art completes its cycle when it's appreciated by someone else. We spend hours and hours making the things we make in the hope that others will see what we've done and take joy from it. We may also hope that the fruits of our creativity bring others some comfort or that sense of "Order in the existential Chaos" we've already talked about. Perhaps we also hope our audience, however big or small, will think better of us as human beings for having made something that moved them. There's nothing wrong with any of this, but for our own sakes we have to untangle our personal neediness from our drive to create, or the emotional waters around our work can get very muddy, very quickly.

&

Let's take a look at the tragic life of Vincent van Gogh.

His life began with a series of brutal rejections.

First, his mother gave birth to Vincent only a year or so after she miscarried a child she had posthumously also named Vincent. He would never live up to his mother's idea of the little angel she had lost and so always felt the lack of that vital and full love only a mother can give.

Second, he would be rebuffed by a series of women he had fallen for, which could only have added to his struggling sense of self-worth.

Third, he had chosen to give his life in service to the church, which had roundly refused him on a number of occasions. He finally got himself work by choosing to serve a poor coal mining community in Borinage, Belgium, where few other clergymen were willing to go. He slept on hard wooden floorboards to give up his bed for others, gave away many of his possessions to those in need, and was called "The Christ of the Coal Mines" by the people he lived amongst. But the church turned its back on him, acting ashamed of his decision to live in squalor with the community he cared for.

It was after leaving the church that he turned his hand to painting in earnest and dared to dream that he could make a living as an artist. I'm sure you can empathise with how much he must have wanted this to work out and how desperately he needed to find acceptance at least in this. However, life is never simple and rarely fair, so instead, he found himself constantly struggling for work and fighting to make ends meet financially. He was only able to feed himself for much of his life because of a stipend generously provided by his loving younger brother Theo, but even so he was often on the verge of absolute poverty. Vincent van Gogh was the epitome of the struggling, starving artist.

In 1888, at the age of 35, he moved to Arles in the south of France, where, inspired by the bright sunshine and vibrant colours of the countryside, his painting output went through the roof. He rented a house to live in and also used the space to found a studio that he hoped would attract other artists and eventually begin a collective.

Paul Gauguin was the only artist who would join him, but after a couple of months of productive collaboration, Vincent became unstable and had a huge argument with Gauguin in which he came after him with a straight razor. The altercation ended with his newfound collaborator fleeing town for his own safety. After chasing Gauguin down the street, Vincent then famously returned to the studio and used the razor on himself to sever his own ear, wrapped it up in newspaper, and delivered it to a local sex worker for "safekeeping."

He constantly struggled with mental illness throughout his life, but after this particular incident the town was concerned about their own safety, so they signed a petition demanding that he be locked up in the local asylum. Vincent eventually had himself admitted, and he sent boxes of his paintings to his family for storage with a letter stating that his career as a painter was never going to materialise. It seemed for a moment that he had given up and was happy just to be locked away.

His younger brother Theo hadn't given up on him though. He arranged for him to have space to keep painting in the Saint-Paul de Mausole asylum, and it was during this season that he produced some of the works we know him best for today, including perhaps his most famous work *The Starry Night*, which he painted whilst looking out of the barred windows of his cell. While Vincent's health began to improve, his brother organised a showing of his work, where a single painting called *The Red Vineyards* sold for 400 francs, but it was bittersweet because all that money went back to Vincent's family to make up a tiny portion of the debt repayments he owed them.

This particular sale is often the painting cited in the apocryphal tale of "Van Gogh only selling one painting in his lifetime." That's almost certainly not accurate, and we do know of a few other small sales that he made, but the point of the oft-recited tale stands: that his dream was to become a recognised and successful painter in his lifetime, and in comparison to his contemporaries Toulouse-Lautrec, Gauguin, Pissarro, and Monet, he was an abject failure who sold almost no work, received unkind reviews, and was never taken seriously by the art world.

He continued to paint and was eventually deemed well enough to leave the asylum. His family organised a place for him to stay in the countryside just outside Paris, and he carried on painting in the hopes that his work would eventually be recognised and appreciated for what it was. However, he couldn't find an audience for his art, and he continued to struggle financially.

The rejections of his work and concerns over being a burden to his brother eventually overwhelmed him on July 27, 1890. He walked a couple of miles out of town to paint in the fields, as was his custom, but at some point decided instead to take a revolver and shoot himself in the chest. He botched the job and ended up stumbling back to town, only to die in his bed two days later, with his loving brother Theo by his bedside.

This is the same Vincent van Gogh who is now considered by some to be the greatest painter of all time. His work sells for exorbitant sums; for example, in 1990, his painting *Portrait of*

Doctor Gachet sold for $82.5 million. People all over the world study his work, and more than 2.1 million people travel to visit the impressive Van Gogh Museum in Amsterdam every year to stand in front of his physical works in person.

What a devastating story. Perhaps the greatest artist of all time was subject to rejection after rejection, and I believe he was just desperately looking to belong, like the rest of us. He created over 900 pieces over his short 10-year career as an artist from 1880-1890. He was driven by a belief in his talent but was eventually defeated by a combination of mental illness and despair. I'm no psychologist, but when I hear his story, I can feel the intense pain of a gifted person who was rejected and rebuffed over and over again and finally lost hope, with tragic consequences.

There is a simple lesson I learn from Vincent: if the greatest artist of all time couldn't find acceptance for his work in his lifetime, I shouldn't expect to be owed anything more than the struggles he endured. That means, if I want to stay inspired and avoid losing hope, I need to learn from his story and teach myself to deal with my own desperate need for approval and acceptance before it robs me of my motivation, or derails me altogether. The hard truth is that not all art will complete its cycle. In fact, the majority of things human beings make likely won't reach an appreciative audience, and so we need to calibrate our expectations early, or we may give up making altogether.

&

There are lots of different ways we look for attention as artists, but writing in 2021 we can't talk about this issue of "attention" without addressing the ubiquitous phenomenon of social media. So let's use this uniquely 21st-century problem as a lens through which to focus on our collective struggles to find appreciation for our work.

Artists today are tempted to chase adulation and acceptance like never before, and the explosion of online sharing makes this a more complicated issue to navigate than perhaps at any other time in human history.

It's important to acknowledge that the Internet and social media are a gift. Not so long ago, the only way to get any eyeballs on the work we were producing was to be at the very top of the recognised pool of talent and then be taken on by agents, patrons, and art dealers who would help us put on exhibitions or recitals of the art we were engaged in. Obviously, that route only worked out for a very tiny proportion of painters, writers, and performers who were either extraordinarily talented or unfeasibly lucky, leaving the vast majority of makers unappreciated and undiscovered.

However, the creative world has been democratised like never before with the advent of the Internet. You no longer need to be the very best at what you do in order to build an audience around your work. You have the potential of loading your work online for the waiting world to see and appreciate, entirely on your own initiative. People from the other side of the globe whom you will likely never meet in person can comment and interact with you around the work you are sharing.

You also have Follow and Subscribe buttons that people can use to declare not just their interest in what you're doing now but also what you might do in the future. Knowing that there are people out there who are following your work can be hugely encouraging and motivating.

Funding ourselves as artists has changed too. In the medieval world, the very best artists would have their whole lives funded by popes, or kings, or rich merchants who believed in their artistic pursuits. These patrons wanted to make sure that their favourite artist had everything they needed, and in turn, could devote every waking hour to creating the work their patron loved to see. But with the Internet, no matter what level of artist we are, we can build a following and collect a whole stable of "mini patrons," ordinary people who support the work we do through small, regular donations; this means that every "maker of things"—not just the hyper-gifted elite—now has the potential to generate support for their work.

These possibilities are brand-new historically speaking, and because of this incredible innovation, we're seeing a multiplicity of artists finding their smaller, appreciative audiences in unprecedented numbers. So, before you assume I'm about to rail on about the evils of social media, I'm not. As a photographer and filmmaker in the digital age, I personally use the technological tools at my disposal every day to build a following around the things I make, and as things stand today, I am fortunate enough to be able to support myself thanks to the engaged audience I've managed to build online. I still find it a little surreal that I can post an image I've made, or share a short film I've produced, and within minutes I have people from Malaysia to Moldova, and from Chile to China, view that work and share their appreciation. However, as heady a notion as that is, our expectations around the acceptance or attention we receive online have the power to knock our Ego off-balance and derail us if we don't maintain a healthy perspective.

Social media can also cause artists a great deal of misery. Choosing to share our work is no guarantee of success, or fame, or fortune. I'm not one of those snake oil salesmen who pretends to know how to crack the algorithms. I've tried various things in the past that went nowhere, and to be very frank, I still don't really understand why whatever I'm doing at the moment is working. I'm also aware that this audience I've built could evaporate tomorrow for countless reasons, so I take it all with a pinch of salt. Again, producing work I'm proud of is within my power, but any level of sustained "success" online is completely out of my control, as discussed in the previous chapter.

This perspective is so important to get into our heads these days because, without it, a lot of artists struggle with anxiety, many walking away altogether from the thing they love. I've seen what this struggle does to people. I personally know fellow photographers who are so angry they aren't getting the attention online they believe they deserve that it's souring their love of the art form. They are constantly uploading, waiting for the love to pour in, and then deleting their accounts in protest because the world online isn't giving them what they expect. They are writing long blog posts about how awful particular social media platforms are, almost making it a moral issue in an attempt to disguise their own anger and jealousy. If at all possible, I want to save you from that by encouraging you to mentally separate your love of "making" from the capricious social media game.

Online platforms are just tools. They aren't good or bad; they're just full of human beings who are using them in ways that suit them best. Most people aren't using them to intelligently review your art and reward you for your brilliance. Statistically speaking, most people are using them selfishly for quick, bite-sized entertainment, and you and I are no different if we're honest. In fact, if you're a regular user of social media, I'm going to guess some things about you:

I would guess you've subscribed to a lot of channels on YouTube over the years, but you don't really watch the videos posted there any more because you're constantly discovering new channels and moving on to new things.

I'll presume that you've hit that Follow button on many independent musicians on Spotify with the best of intentions to keep up with their output, but you usually go back to playing the same limited playlist of favourites that you know is guaranteed to lift your mood.

I would imagine you follow a mixed bag of people on platforms like Instagram, not because you find their photography inspiring to look at but more broadly because you think they're interesting people for one reason or another, and you want to keep up-to-date with what they're doing.

Now, if I'm right and we can all admit this about ourselves, then we have to recognise that everyone else uses the Internet in the same way we do. Most interaction online is momentary and very surface-level in nature. That's not wrong; it's just how most human beings choose to use the Internet on any given day. Keeping that in mind will save us from allowing unrealistic expectations to build, or from putting our heart on the line when we share our work with the world.

In my case, I have a fair number of followers and subscribers on platforms like Instagram and YouTube, but I don't put undue stock in that, and the reason is simple: I know well that online popularity doesn't signify mastery.

The danger of social media is that we get fixated on numbers as if they exist as some sort of "talent score." We make a big mistake when we assume that the higher the number and the more attention we are getting for our work online, the better we are as artists.

But for those of you who are determined to chase the big numbers regardless, I'm going to crack the Internet for you and share the secret to "social media success." Are you ready? If you want a big following online, get naked or get a puppy. People seem pretty fond of both, and if you create accounts sharing the relative joys of either, I imagine that you'll have an interested following in no time at all. However, if you follow this advice and achieve that big number you crave, know that the size of your newfound audience doesn't mean that you suddenly became a great artist.

&

You see, at some point we have to choose what's important to us.

The work of developing your skills, digging deep in your understanding of your chosen art form, and growing into a human being with important things to say is all work that is separate from the online numbers game. The sad fact is that your average Internet user doesn't recognise this deeper work because they just won't spend enough time with the things you've made, so they can never be a reliable judge of the depth you're building.

It's easy to prove this to myself as a photographer. If I have a sizable following online and that following equates to my talent as an artist, then why aren't galleries calling me up and begging me to showcase my work with them? It's obvious, isn't it? They know how to judge the quality of the photography itself, and they aren't swayed in the slightest by the collective opinions of the online masses.

I'm also not fooling other great photographers with my "numbers." My heroes, such as Salgado and Meyerowitz, McCurry and Leibovitz, aren't hanging around in my comment sections treating me like a peer, because I'm not. I didn't fool them into thinking I'm their equal just because there are particular numbers attached to my online accounts. They know better than that, and so do I. I have a long way to go, and that's the way it should be if I'm really serious about being the best photographer, or filmmaker, or writer I can be.

The fact is that I know photographers infinitely superior to me with a fraction of my online audience, and I also know beginner photographers with little experience who have massive followings. I know cats with online followings that dwarf us all, so can we admit that those numbers mean very little and stop taking them so seriously?

If you're an accomplished painter, you'll know about the greats who came before you and what made them special. None of you who've been at this for a while will be fooled by the big YouTube channels teaching painting techniques to millions of subscribers. You'll look beyond the numbers and judge the work for yourself.

If you're a dancer, you'll know about the history of movement and whose broad shoulders you now dance upon. You aren't easily impressed by the millions of views on a TikTok dance video because you know how to look for quality in the movement itself.

If you're a poet, you'll have the greats sitting on your bookshelf, and you'll know the descriptive heights that can be reached by true masters. You'll look beyond the number of followers on an Instagram poet's work to the structure and finesse of their writing, all the while weighing that against everything you've learnt from those who came before you.

We all look for quality, and if we're in the know, then no one's social media numbers are going to fool us. That's not to say that these people aren't talented, or even a future "great," but you know enough not to be swayed by the numbers and to look at the work itself.

The same is true for you. The only people who will be impressed with your following online will be beginners. It's always, and only, recognition from those coming up the ladder behind you. I'm not suggesting there's anything wrong with that. It feels good to inspire those who are dipping their toes into our art form, but if we're serious about getting good at what we do, then surely it serves us to put no stock in the online numbers game and to set our sights higher. Personally, I want the people who really know about photography to think I'm doing good work, and I want photographers who are better than I am to think I'm doing something worthwhile. That's the affirmation I take seriously; everything else is just noise.

For your own sake and sanity, stop chasing online attention. Focus instead on being the best you possibly can at what you do, and remember that the Internet's collective opinion is not a reliable indicator of how you're doing. The Internet is a million miles wide but often only an inch deep, so for me social media will never be my yardstick. Becoming an artist of any worth has to be a real-world pursuit and the work of a lifetime, so don't let this empty chase distract you from that deeper work.

&

Ultimately, the choice comes down to "pleasing the masses" or "growing as a creator."

Let me give you an example. I know people particularly love the high-contrast black-and-white images I post to platforms like Instagram, especially if they feature a hard diagonal shadow. They're "crowd-pleaser" images that score well in the social media game, meaning they get lots of "likes," and "shares," and "comments," and other yummy online treats. But honestly, I'm getting bored with those shots. These are the types of photographs I can take on any sunny day, and they are no longer a challenge. I want to move away from this cliché of my own making and toward discovering new things.

Now, if attention were my goal, I would just keep taking the same images and riding that affirmation as long as the Internet keeps feeding me disembodied "likes," but in the process, I would completely stall my own growth as a photographer.

But if growth as a photographer is my goal, I have to explore new things whether people "get it" or not. In all likelihood, I won't be very good at whatever new direction I attempt, at least initially, and branching out to pursue new avenues may cost me some attention. In fact, I started making a shift in the work I share online about a year ago, and I had to forfeit the usual compliments for some very unkind comments from people who couldn't understand what I was doing and why I wasn't sharing the images they loved. Some even acted entitled and said things like, "I didn't follow you for this sort of thing. I'm unfollowing," as if I owed them, or worked for them somehow. Regardless, I knew I had to mix things up and embrace the fact that I would suck for a while because I knew that exploration and struggle would lead to new growth and direction in the long run.

Similarly, I get criticised all the time for the films I post on YouTube. "They are too long." "You talk too much." "The pace is too slow." I don't care, though, because I promised myself that if I were going to engage on a platform like YouTube it wouldn't be to play the numbers game. It would be to create the sort of videos I wanted to see more of. I was well aware that this approach wouldn't suit the short attention span of the average YouTube user, but they weren't my target audience and big numbers were never my goal.

This is true not only for style in my case but content as well. I have about 100 videos on my channel, and only a handful mention cameras or lenses. Most of the videos I post are focussed more on the "why" of photography than the "how" because that's what interests me. I knew starting out that there were loads of channels out there giving gear reviews or "top ten tips" lists, and I didn't want to be another tutorial or review channel. Of course, there's nothing wrong with channels that focus on that sort of thing; it's just that I wanted to push a little deeper. That said, on the odd occasion when I do mention a particular camera in the course of a video, or if I produce a practical tutorial, those videos do much better in the social media numbers game.

The implications are clear: if I want my channel to grow big, and fast, I could simply switch topics and provide practical information to those who are shopping for cameras or trying to develop their skills. There would be absolutely nothing wrong with that, except that it would mean that I am no longer producing films I believe in. Even though my decision to make more thoughtful films will probably mean that I reach a plateau of viewers sooner than other channels— because there are always going to be a limited number of people with the patience to endure my ramblings—I will also be able to sleep at night because I'm doing something I care about, and that's really important to me.

This is one of the things that impresses me about van Gogh; although he lost his battles at the end, it seems that he refused to change his work to become more "palatable" and "salable" for the art market because he believed in what he was doing, even if the general public thought it too bold and garish. The lack of affirmation his work received may have contributed to his eventual loss of hope, but it never caused him to compromise his work—another important lesson I take from his life.

Do you see the danger of letting this "numbers game" thinking sink in? If we buy the lie that online attention means we've arrived, we may stop developing altogether if we ever achieve it. We may start to convince ourselves that we've plumbed the depths of our talent and hit a seam of gold when in reality we've merely scratched the surface and found a gimmick that won us some attention from the masses. At that point, we will have stagnated, our conscience would be drowned out by the cheers of our fans, and we will have never become what we could have been.

Ask yourself why you're engaging on the platforms you are. You don't have to. No one's forcing you, so what's the real reason? Maybe the most practical way to start is by asking yourself how much attention is enough, and what is its purpose? What are your specific goals?

My reason for engaging online is simple: I want to be able to support myself as an artist. I want to build a small core of followers who believe in what I'm doing enough to support me in my work. I said upfront that we live in an amazing time when, as artists, we have the potential to build our own viable stables of mini-patrons who can sustain us, and the number of supporters we need to keep our heads above water might not be as big as you think.

Before starting my YouTube channel, I had thankfully read the now-infamous blog post by Kevin Kelly called "1000 True Fans," which really helped me to set realistic goals. Here's how his article begins:

To be a successful creator you don't need millions. You don't need millions of dollars or millions of customers, millions of clients or millions of fans. To make a living as a craftsperson, photographer, musician, designer, author, animator, app maker, entrepreneur, or inventor you need only thousands of true fans.

Kelly goes on to describe a "true fan" as anyone who is willing to buy your work, to support you with regular donations, to buy tickets when you come to town, to purchase your merch, or to commission you for custom pieces. Now, the specific math varies widely depending on what you do and where in the world you do it, but the point is that it's possible to build that small supportive core who will sustain you in your work.

After 15 years as a full-time photographer, I'm grateful to be able to say that I've been successfully working for myself for the last three years, not as a freelancer working for clients but rather by making the work I love with support from my core followers. Don't get me wrong; I'm grateful for everyone who expresses an interest in my work, whether they support me financially or not, but my practical goal wasn't to amass an inflated subscriber number signifying people who are vaguely interested in something I did once. It was always to build that small core audience that would help make what I'm doing sustainable.

You may assume that you need that huge following in order to have that small engaged and supportive core and that it's always a stable percentage of a much bigger whole, but if you build with purpose from the start, that isn't necessarily true. An artist with 1,500 people following their work may already have enough true fans supporting them to make a living, but an artist with 2 million subscribers may be struggling to get any true fans to support their work. By focussing on quality over quantity and establishing clear goals upfront, you can set yourself up to begin building a stronger following and better chance at a more sustainable career.

Whether online or in our flesh-and-blood reality, it's important to get honest with ourselves about our expectations and face our need for approval head-on. If we're in this for the long haul, then in my mind we can't take it seriously enough. We make the most devastating error when we assume that attention for our work can fulfill us, or heal us, or fill the holes in our souls. If we needed any proof of this, we need only look at the other end of the spectrum from van Gogh to see a long list of people who found huge levels of fame and still lost hope. From Mark Rothko to Kurt Cobain, from Robin Williams to Kate Spade, we have a clear message that attention cannot heal us or give us hope.

I've been to counselling sessions many times in order to un-pack my own neediness, and I've sat in many leather chairs, talking to the stern and silent faces of psychologists about my own story to try to better understand my responses. I learned to face the hole my absent father left in my heart, and I faced all the embarrassing ways I tried to push older men to be my surrogate father and how every appropriate boundary they put up felt like a new rejection. I identified the ways this feeling and fear of abandonment had seeped into my relationships and given me an unnecessarily de-fensive edge because I was constantly expecting the worst. But most importantly, I was able to acknowledge the heavy weight of expectation I put on the amount of attention I got for my music, my photography, my filmmaking, my writing, or whatever I happened to be engaged in at the time, and the lies I believed about how it would make me whole when it reached a certain level.

Knowing my own story and recognising the shunned little boy's voice when he gets angry that he isn't being accepted yet again—and even making friends with him—was the key for me. As crazy as it sounds, I even talk to him sometimes. When I feel that fear and anger surface because I'm hurt by the mean things someone has said about something I've made, or I'm disappointed that no one cares about the last piece I've put out, I'll picture the little boy I used to be and remind him, "This isn't about you. You are still as valuable as everyone else around you, and you are doing your best. Some people will like what you do, and some people won't. How could it be any other way? None of this, either good or bad, speaks to your value as a human being. You are good as you are."

If I end up asking my art to make up for my emotional shortfalls, I won't make it. "Dealing with my pain" and "becoming a good artist" have to be separate pursuits, and neither can be significantly aided by something as frivolous and fluffy as "online attention."

Maybe you're reading this and realising how you've lost focus and been seduced by this drive for attention. Great, because realising it is the first and biggest step to getting beyond it. The second is to remind ourselves why we make in the first place.

In 2007, writer John Maloof bought an anonymous box of negatives at a Chicago auction as part of research he was doing on Portage Park. When he began to scan the negatives and convert them to positives, he realised that he had stumbled on the work of an exceptional street photographer. He posted the images online and received an overwhelming response from people praising the quality of the work and asking who this person was. With a bit of digging, John discovered that the photographer had been a nanny named Vivian Maier, and over the next few years, he would try and track down as much of her work as he could, ultimately finding and interviewing people who knew her for his 2013 documentary, *Finding Vivian Maier.*

It's clear from watching the documentary and hearing from those who knew her that Vivian was a complicated figure. However, what was simple about her was that she absolutely loved to take photographs. The world of photography was her compulsive "happy place."

What I found so confounding about her, though, as a fellow photographer, was that she seemed to find joy in the act of photographing alone and not necessarily from the results. For me, the joy of photography derives not just from the taking of the images but especially from seeing the final results and sharing them with others. But when those boxes were discovered at auction, they were filled with undeveloped rolls of film, which means that she never saw many of her own images. Perhaps the reason was something as practical as not being able to afford the development costs, but that doesn't fully explain it, because if she could afford to keep buying film, why not invest in the development and cut back on the shooting? She was making a choice; the act of taking images was infinitely more important to her than seeing the final results. She had already wrung the joy out of the process just by being out on the street with her camera, watching, setting her exposure, composing her frames, and snapping the shutter. She was making all the time and seemed unconcerned with either the final images or the attention her work may or may not receive.

Similarly, Garry Winogrand was a famous street photographer who died in 1984, and at the time of his death, over 2,500 rolls of undeveloped film were discovered in his home.

Winograd was famous for not taking himself or his work too seriously and being playful toward and dismissive of those who tried to add layers of deep interpretation to his images. He once simply said, "I don't have anything to say in any picture. My only interest in photography is to see what something looks like as a photograph." There was an uncomplicated joy in his act of making that was just about the process, and he didn't seem to allow himself to become overly concerned with our collective opinions or complicated interpretations of his work.

What if, like these photographers, we could learn to get our satisfaction from the act of making itself instead of everyone else's response to it? What if we could wean ourselves off our addiction to attention and become more self-contained, returning to doing what we do for the simple love of it?

What if I could take you into your future and show you how things would turn out for you? What if we stepped through a portal and I could show you your aged self, still painting, still writing, still drawing, still designing, still photographing? What if you had found no substantial fame for your work? Would you be disappointed? What if you looked closer and noticed that your older self was smiling deeply as they scratched away with that pencil on the paper, or pounded away at that keyboard? What if you looked at the work and were taken aback by how good it now was, how it had matured into something solid, something you could be incredibly proud of?

What if, on top of all this, you realised that you had found ways to sustain yourself in the making, right into your old age, and it seemed that somewhere along the road you gave up that reach for infamy and contented yourself in the making alone? Would you still rush to the computer to check the online "score," or would you be satisfied with the joy and freedom of expression you had attained? Would that be enough to make you happy?

That's my abiding hope for you, and for me: that we learn to separate out our need for affirmation from the joy we derive from making. That we learn to love ourselves first, to deal with our pain well, and then make for the joy of making and perhaps to bring a little Order to someone else's Chaos.

Who knows what happens with your work later? Maybe nothing. Maybe like van Gogh, you were onto something that people just weren't ready for yet, but thank goodness you found a way to keep going and didn't give up, because future generations will now benefit.

What if the very best that happens is that your work touches the lives of a precious few, but that ends up giving you a deep and abiding sense of fulfilment? Well, that seems like a great way to spend a life.

So create vibrantly and vigorously, and if you're lucky, within your lifetime you will see people appreciate what you do. I can't guarantee how many will come or what their response will be. No one can. But I hope you can get yourself to a place where that doesn't really matter. I hope you can reach a point within yourself where you are so fulfilled by the work you are producing that everything else, including the response you get, is just a bonus. If you can, I believe you will save yourself, preserve your motivation, and perhaps ironically give yourself the best chance of developing your unique voice and finding an audience who truly cares.

Envy

It's 1998, I'm 20 years old, and I'm sitting in the hot sun in a field of dry, brown grass in front of a truck. It's no ordinary truck though. This one has expanded itself, Transformers-style, into a fully equipped stage, complete with lights and sound system.

At present, a band is playing. The crowd is loving their performance, but I am quietly seething.

You see, my band has just been up there, and we had a bunch of technical difficulties. The monitor speakers were down, so all we could really hear from our vantage point were unshielded drums, so it was impossible to hear our own playing. As a result, I knew my pitch had been off, and our playing as a band had been sloppy.

Between sets, though, the crew had fixed the issue and the band on stage at the moment were, well, brilliant. The drum and bass combo were tight, the guitarist's licks were intricate and accurate, and the lead singer had more charisma than I would ever be able to muster, not to mention an outstanding voice. The more I watched, the harder it was to blame our apparent shortcomings on faulty speakers.

If I were honest with myself, which I didn't feel like being, I knew that the way the crowd had suddenly perked up when this new band had started playing could only be explained by the fact that they were much better than we were. Festival crowds don't scream for technical problems being fixed; they scream for great music.

On top of it all, this was a battle of the bands. It was a deliberate competition, and I knew we were outclassed, outperformed—just out of the running altogether.

I sat there picking dried grass, twisting it in my fingers, I was trying to mentally pick and poke holes into anything I could in their performance. I was getting mean too, as my internal criticism started to extend to their looks. "That guy's haircut is so stupid. He's trying too hard. He must be a nightmare off stage. Imagine having to live with him."

My chance to play well was gone; all I had left was a childish game of attempting to bring them down in my head, down to my low and miserable level. They were, of course, oblivious, lost in the adulation of an adoring crowd, swept up in the exhilarating feeling of a band in sync. My angst was my own private little hell.

It took the bass player in our band to break the spell. He was a lanky, gentle giant who had been watching the same thing I had, but he suddenly piped up and said, "They're really good, aren't they?"

I turned on him wordlessly, obviously looking a little incredulous.

Confused at my expression, he simply said, "What? They are, aren't they?"

I suddenly felt very ashamed. Of course they were. It's why I was angry, and his beautifully generous and completely unthreatened attitude made me feel very small and ugly.

&

It's strange, isn't it, that we can often appreciate an art form until the minute we participate in it ourselves? Suddenly, it becomes a competition which can sour our whole attitude.

Imagine the following scenario.

You discover you love looking at painted portraits, so you begin taking regular trips to the National Portrait Gallery on weekends just to wander around admiring the beautiful work on display from some of the world's most talented artists, in awe of their ability to capture some unspoken essence of their subjects, each in their own inimitable styles.

But then you dare to dream. You wonder to yourself, *Maybe I could paint*. So you buy a set of paints, take some classes, and start to produce portraits of your own. You go through all the usual stages from despairing about how awful you are to getting some encouragement from your tutors, to starting to get a handle on some of the techniques, and with a great deal of courage and perseverance, you find yourself progressing.

A year later, you are getting pretty good. You practice on your friends and family, and they give you some great feedback, showering praise on your development. Your friends even start referring to you as an "artist," sharing your work around and showing off on your behalf.

You build a little following online of people who think your work is great. You even book a professional review with a local gallery and they say some very nice things about a few of your pieces and let you know that they would love to hang your work in their space sometime soon.

One day you're strolling past the National Portrait Gallery, and you realise that you haven't visited for a long time. Work has been busy, and you are spending all your free time working on your own paintings now. So you decide to pop in on the spur of the moment, but you quickly discover that something has changed. You look at the paintings differently now. You no longer have the wide-eyed appreciation of a punter, but the slightly removed and critical eye of a would-be competitor.

You know they are great works of art, but you have changed. You are now on the playing field. You're proud of the progress you've made and excited by the possibility that you may receive this level of recognition one day. You even find yourself paying less attention to the art on the walls than on previous visits because you are daydreaming about your own work hanging there.

You also notice some ugly thoughts surfacing. You're looking for holes in the work you once loved unconditionally.

There is maybe even, if you're very honest, a low-level, broiling jealousy.

Make no mistake; envy is one of the emotions that can both ruin our enjoyment of the journey and hamstring our growth as an artist unless we get a handle on it early, and the place to start is recognising it for what it is when it surfaces.

⅋

It comes down to emotional intelligence.

Being an emotionally intelligent person is different from being a very emotional person. You can be very outwardly emotional or very emotionally reserved but have a high level of emotional intelligence in either case.

Emotional intelligence is about being present with our emotions and able to quickly and accurately assess why they are there and what we need to be paying attention to. However, so many of us haven't yet learned how to speak their language. This is most often because we are unwilling to look at ourselves and would rather point the finger at those around us to explain why we feel what we're feeling. However, taking that route will, more often than not, render us none the wiser as to the true cause of our feelings and could lead to destructive patterns and bitterness.

Let's consider a quick example most of us have experienced.

You are driving home from work in busy traffic, and some guy cuts you off with his car.

You're fuming mad!

"How dare he?"

"He almost hit my car."

"Who does he think he is?"

"We all have to get home, mate. You're no more important than the rest of us."

"What a #!*$!"

I've been there—most of us have. But the fact is that we don't really know whether that guy who cut us off even noticed us. Some people are just bad drivers, after all, but my emotional response is as strong as it would have been if I believed his careless driving was a deliberate insult, directed at me personally. But whether I'm dealing with someone who was trying to rush home and made a knowingly cheeky manoeuvre with his car, or whether he didn't even notice the inconvenience he was causing me, my strong emotional response probably isn't proportional to the act.

The emotionally intelligent among you will know this in the moment. You may still have the initial emotional knee-jerk response, but you can also probably have a giggle to yourself in the car about how heated you got over such a little thing. If you have that self-awareness, you will then start asking yourself questions to work out what that response was really about.

With a bit of honesty, you may do a quick internal inventory and realise that your response was really about anger over your perceived powerlessness.

Maybe you're angry because your job isn't going well, and your boss is domineering in his demands, and you feel powerless to stand up for yourself.

Maybe you're struggling in your relationship with your partner, and you feel as if you're losing your sense of self in your relationship.

Maybe you've just moved to this city from a more peaceful part of the world, and you're struggling with how much time and space is being taken from you in this new context.

Maybe it's all these things combining to leave you feeling invisible, lonely, and powerless over your own journey.

Now, suddenly, you realise that your anger at this guy's thoughtless action is a symptom of a much bigger problem, which better explains the intensity of that feeling, and, if you face it, may mean you're able to find solutions for it.

But too often many of us experience a negative emotion and lazily jump to finding someone or something else to blame it on, and then stop questioning because we don't want to look at ourselves. Our lack of honesty and awareness will rob us of the ability to deal with the real problem so we remain frustrated, and if this pattern continues, it will get even worse over time. We might lose touch with ourselves completely.

This is why people become bitter—because they get caught in a cycle of blaming and never take an honest look inward. The frustration and anger mount, and the keys to their freedom move farther and farther out of reach.

The truth is that a negative emotion in us, more often than not, is pointing to something about ourselves that needs to change, and it won't go away until we deal with it.

That's obviously not to say that there aren't genuine moments in our lives when someone hurts us and we legitimately feel pain in response to their behaviour, but overly negative emotions are often about something within ourselves that we need to address and it's always worth taking the time to look inward and ask some tough questions.

&

So, with that in mind, let's look at envy.

Envy isn't an emotion we often admit to feeling. We hide it in other emotions so that we don't have to face it in ourselves because we're aware that it isn't an attractive quality. So let's name some of our emotional responses that, if we're honest, probably speak to our jealousy of someone else's talent or success.

How about a feeling of superiority? We have already spoken about this in the chapter on Ego and know that the Ego's greatest trick is to try and make us feel separate from and superior to those around us. However, when this shifts from a general game our mind plays to an obsession with how we are separate from and superior to another artist in particular, that is jealousy hiding in there.

Sometimes we find ourselves applying reductive labelling to other people's work in order to diminish it in our own minds—or the minds of others.

"Yes, I like so-and-so's street photography, but it's really just a version of what Saul Leiter was doing years ago."

"His songwriting is OK, but it's pretty derivative and unimaginative country music at the end of the day."

"Her paintings aren't bad, but honestly, they are just pale imitations of Lucian Freud's work."

Applying labels and placing things in neat boxes is always reductive, and when we find ourselves obsessed with labelling and boxing the work of others, it's a fairly sure sign that envy is lurking there.

A common practice you may have observed online is where people take advantage of the anonymity the Internet provides and act on the need to correct or criticise when no one asked for their opinion. If you find yourself hanging out on other people's profiles, needing to tell them they "exposed that photo incorrectly," that their "poems lack structure," that their "songwriting isn't up to scratch," then you need to ask yourself why. What's driving you to do that, and why these individuals in particular? Is it really because you want to see them get better at what they do, or is it because you are trying to discourage them and act as if you know better? A little self-awareness and emotional intelligence could uncover some jealousy in you that needs to be addressed.

Another place our envy can hide is in our feelings of offence, or our moralisations. If we find ourselves trying to unearth some practice or norm that has been broken by someone's work, it's usually just a cheap trick we're using to attempt to bring them down a peg. We know objectively that it isn't our job to police other artists and make sure they are doing things "correctly." Our only business is our own integrity. However, when we can't help but apply our morality to the work of another artist, it's time to employ some emotional intelligence and face some internal ugliness.

Let me give you an example.

I think a lot of photographers would like to attempt street photography but are justifiably scared. It's an intimidating pursuit. I shared some of my own struggles with it in earlier chapters. Now, imagine a photographer without the courage to head out and try it for themselves looking on at successful street photographers receiving critical acclaim for their work. Jealousy of their perceived success may lead an emotionally unintelligent person to start devising reasons why the whole genre of street photography is "morally bankrupt" (a phrase I have actually heard from one such photographer) to mask their envy, even from themselves.

They may start doing the rounds online of those street photographers receiving attention for their work and jumping into the comments sections of their best candid images of strangers in the street to suggest that not getting their written permission is somehow unethical, or even illegal. Of course, it's neither, certainly not in this country as I write this, and street photography has been a legitimate genre from the earliest days of the medium.

What's interesting to note, though, is that these frustrated fellow photographers aren't criticising the work of Henri Cartier-Bresson, or Joel Meyerowitz, or Elliott Erwitt, or any of the other great street photographers. They also aren't criticising lesser-known street photographers who are receiving little to no attention. They are criticizing their peers who have some buzz around their work. This specificity should be a sign to us that it's not about principle. It's become selective moralising born of jealousy toward a photographer who has something they want.

They would love to be taking images with the same visual interest, but out of fear, they have chosen instead to formulate a moral story in which they are the principled hero "fighting the good fight" without ever having to take risks themselves. In place of picking up a camera and walking out the door, they are at the very least trying to muddy the waters around the work their peers are producing, or at worst, they are trying to get them to stop altogether.

But it's important to remember that what drew them in the first place was the quality of the work or the attention it was receiving.

Feeling entitled to something another artist has, especially attention, is another sign that envy is at work. How often do we think to ourselves something like:

"Why does she have so many people following her work, and I don't?"

"My work should be hanging in this gallery. It's better than theirs."

"Why did that journalist interview him and not me?"

"That website featured her poetry and not mine? But she's rubbish!"

You are owed none of that stuff in the first place, and thinking that the world is a fair place is a big mistake. This is why we spent so much time in the previous chapter talking about managing our need for attention, because if we don't, envy will inevitably follow. To stop our acts of making from turning sour on us, we have to identify this emotion quickly and learn to instinctively whip around to face our own neediness instead of looking for someone else to blame.

♂

Ultimately, envy, just like perfectionism and neediness, is fuelled by some very real fears.

Fear that I'm falling behind.

Fear that I'm not good enough.

Fear that I'm not as talented as others.

Fear that I will not be able to achieve what others have.

Fear of failure.

Maybe even a fear of success that sees us self sabotaging and then attacking those who could graciously accept their successes in ways we couldn't.

You'll notice that all of these fears are comparison fears. They exist because we are constantly weighing ourselves against someone else's talent, or progress, or recognition, or achievements.

Theodore Roosevelt famously said, "Comparison is the thief of joy." We know it well. We experience great excitement about an art form when we first start out, working out the intricacies of the medium and feeling the elation when we start to gain enough control to express what's in our hearts. But we also know that the minute we start to compare our work to the work others are producing, things can sour fast.

I don't think many of us can just skip over this stage where we start to compare and experience jealousy. We're all human, and these are all normal human emotions. The trick is to identify this stage the minute it pops up in our journey, and with the best of our emotional intelligence, call it what it is. We are fearful. We get jealous. When that stage comes, it's a sign that participation in this art form means something to us now. It's become important. Our identity might be getting wrapped up in it. We want to stand out in this field as much as possible, we want to succeed and be recognized, and if we're honest, we want to be better than everyone else.

But when envy comes knocking, remember this: true masters blinker themselves and run their own race.

As we've already discussed, we have never had to be more aware of this tendency than in our age of social media and the Internet. We now have access to everything and are constantly being shown what everyone else is producing.

If you're a photographer, for example, you are seeing thousands of images online every day—not only those of your peers who are producing work alongside you, but you also have access to images from the greats, going back to the beginning of photography itself. Within minutes of a meandering Google search, I can see street images of Paris in the 1950s taken by Cartier-Bresson, the last cover that Annie Leibovitz shot for *Vanity Fair*, portraits taken by Edward Curtis of the Native American tribes at the turn of the last century, or work a friend of mine produced in the last week in my own city.

How could we realistically treat this as a competition when we have access to billions of images taken over the last 200 years of photography? I'm all for having ambition, but it has to be kept in check or it will cause emotional confusion that will ultimately drain us of our energy to create.

We will start running after a thousand different targets and end up making a mess of our growth trying to prove too many points and please the crowd. We will lose all our inspiration because we are no longer looking inward asking ourselves what we really want to say. Instead, we will be too busy looking outward for a way to beat the system and be perceived as better than our rivals.

Make no mistake: envy will take us off track.

But things become very simple when we are disciplined, set ourselves clear and personal targets, and attempt to make the best work we can regardless of what everyone else is up to. Like the best marathon runners, we aren't racing the 1,000 other people taking part on the day. Instead, we are trying to put together the best strategy to run the fastest 26 miles we can personally manage, no matter what everyone else is doing.

We run our own race.

&

Now, none of this means that those feelings of jealousy magically disappear, but I do know one simple and practical action that helps immensely: give the subject of your envy a compliment.

The only reason we find ourselves jealous of someone else is that we know their work is good. So what if, instead of playing jealousy games and harbouring those feelings that will only hold us back, we told that other artist that we think their work is really good?

That day, back at the battle of the bands, was the first time I tried it out. I was so embarrassed by my attitude that I knew I needed to do something, so I forced myself to go and find that band after they had left the stage and tell them how great I thought their set was. I didn't want to, but I knew it was the truth. I suppose I did it as a penance for the ugly things I had been thinking, but I discovered something in the process.

Compliments make envy evaporate.

Even as the words came out of my mouth, I realised I believed everything I was saying. "You guys were great. That second song was brilliant. You have an amazing voice, mate. I just wanted to say well done." I was simply naming the things I was jealous about, but complimenting them made it real and instantly turned jealousy into generosity, and I liked being that human being much more than the bitter man-child who had been twisting grass between his fingers half an hour before. In fact, I suddenly felt very far from that person, farther than 30 minutes should warrant, and I think it's because compliments have a magical ability to break the spell envy casts over us.

Don't believe me? Try it out.

We're usually very frugal with our compliments, and I wonder if it's because we think that giving a compliment means we are admitting we are "less than" someone else because we're still playing the comparison game in our own heads.

In my experience, receiving compliments from greater artists than I hasn't diminished them in my estimation in the slightest. Quite the opposite. When someone I respect reaches out to compliment my work, they become even greater in my eyes because not only do they have the skills that I respected them for in the first place, but they have now revealed themselves to be a gracious, encouraging, secure, and generous human being as well.

If you've had someone in mind as you've been reading this chapter, someone you now realise you are jealous of, you can feel how much effort this action will take. When I initially suggested that you compliment them on their work, you might have thought it absurd when applied to your specific context. I'm not suggesting it will be easy. You will probably have to force yourself to do it, just like I did, but I promise you the results will be profound. It may just set you free and get you back to creating.

As it happened, there were even better bands to come that day, and I had a great time. I enjoyed every one of them. Instead of sitting there feeling angry that we came second to last in the competition, I became a fan of some new musicians and, more importantly, made some new friends.

The overriding memory I have now isn't of my little internal tantrum, or of the disastrous set we had, but of sitting with my bandmates laughing at our technical misfortunes and enjoying great music as the sun set over the distant mountains. The compliment had done its good work, and I had managed to let the competition go. Things immediately became simple once again, and I was just a young man in his twenties who loved to listen to and make music.

Critique

Let me take you back to my dreaded homiletics class in seminary.

I was in my third year, and I had improved by leaps and bounds in my ability to communicate in public. In fact, I started to build a reputation outside of the seminary and found myself invited to different churches in the region on most weekends to appear as a guest speaker. I began to feel like the ecclesiastical version of a rock star, which is as sad as it sounds but at the time it felt great.

A couple of years in, those homiletics classes weren't actually that "dreaded" anymore. In fact, I looked forward to them because the criticism of my first year had by now been replaced with regular compliments in my third year.

On the particular day in question, I walked in with a message I had been working on for a while. I was confident in it. I thought I had some very clever ideas in there, some engaging stories that I knew would land as intended, and I felt as though the content of my talk was masterfully riding the line between orthodoxy and innovation.

For the first 45 minutes, I delivered the talk I had prepared; then we were released for a short break as usual and returned for the critique. I was no longer nervous about these sessions. My Ego had over-calibrated for my lack of confidence a while ago and now had me thinking that I was "separate and superior" to most of the people in the room. In all honesty, I didn't feel they had much to tell me anymore, so I usually sat back absorbing the compliments and quietly finding reasons to dismiss the odd criticism.

The compliments flowed in as expected, without a single criticism, for the first 30 minutes of the session. However, our lecturer had been sitting quietly at the back of the class the whole time, not saying a word.

His name was Vic, and I deeply respected him. He was the man I wanted to grow into one day. He was intensely thoughtful, caring, and singular in his approach to teaching. He had a unique style of lecturing, which usually saw him enter with a stack of books, each bookmarked with so many large scraps of roughly torn paper that he sometimes looked like a man who had just retrieved his little library from a pile of pale leaf litter. He would walk in, sit on the edge of his desk, and touch his finger to his lips, deep in thought. Sometimes, he would sit like that for a full minute, leaving the room in silence while we, in turn, waited uneasily for the awkward space to be filled and the lesson to begin. Sometimes, the silence was broken only when he would look at us, frown, and say, "You know, I don't know where to start today."

Then he might tell us a story about someone he saw on his walk to the seminary that morning.

He might then pick up a book from his stack, and read an excerpt to us.

Then he might have asked the class a question to get us contributing before he launched into another story.

When you were in the middle of these lectures, it was rarely clear how all these things connected, but we had learnt to be patient.

His seemingly random start to each session, combined with his rambling approach to working out what to talk about next, might justifiably leave the uninitiated thinking that this man was just winging it and was perennially unprepared. However, minutes before the bell to end each class, Vic would drop one magical sentence and let it hang in the air, and suddenly every seemingly disparate story, quote, reading, and question he had laid about snapped into clarity. A single mind-altering perspective or thought, which would require days to chew on in order to plumb its depths, was left in the place of everything that came before it.

On his best days, he seemed like a magician to me, and every piece of the trick, viewed in hindsight, now appeared entirely necessary and in its rightful place. You might wonder, as I did initially, if it was all an act, but one visit to his book-strewn office confirmed that this meandering method was just his way. It was near impossible to take notes in his lectures or neatly conceptualise what I was learning for the purposes of tests and exams, but I can confidently say that I've never learnt more about life in such a short span of time than when sitting and listening to Vic teach. (It won't be the last time you hear about Vic in this book.)

So, if there were one compliment I valued in that room, it was his, but time was running out and he just sat there, finger characteristically pressed to his lips in thought, listening to the comments from the class.

Finally, when there was a lull in the commentary from my classmates, and only minutes before the class was set to end, he began to speak. "Sean," he said. He followed my name with an implausibly long pause.

"I don't really know what to say."

Another long pause.

Was he so deeply moved by my brilliance that I had rendered him speechless?

Then it came.

"If I'm honest, you insulted me today."

Another long pause.

I was crestfallen. The class was shocked because Vic was always such a kind and encouraging man. He didn't have a bad bone in his body, so my talk must have been really bad for him to say something so pointed. Surely, there was an explanation? Maybe this was a joke, although I don't think I'd ever heard him tell one, so this would be a first.

Then, nothing.

No explanation followed.

He just shook his head and dismissed the class.

I left the room shamefaced and sheepish, a little disorient-ed as to what had just happened. Talking to a few of my classmates afterward, I found that they were as confused and shocked as I was. I got a lot of encouraging pats on the back and people saying things like "I didn't think it was bad at all," "maybe he was just having a bad day," or "maybe he didn't mean it that way."

For the next 24 hours, his comment rang in my ears. I had played dumb with my classmates, but once alone, I had to admit to myself that I had some idea what he may be talk-ing about. Could he have been confirming the same creep-ing suspicion I had been desperately trying to suppress for weeks in my own head, a nagging feeling that I was showing off and losing the substance of what I wanted to say?

The next day, he called me to his office. He sat down with me and said, "Sean, I don't apologise for what I said, but I want to explain why I said it. I acknowledge you have a gift, but I think you've forgotten what it's there for. You were given this ability to help others and not to make yourself look good. Your messages are filling up with gimmicks and stories that are designed to impress, and the good stuff is being pushed out. I think you insult your audiences when you do that, and you demean yourself as well. I don't want to see you do that anymore. I hope you understand, Sean, I wouldn't have said what I did yesterday to a lot of students, but I said it to you, not because I have something against you—just the opposite. I said it because I really believe in what you could be, and I don't want to see you settle for this."

I knew he was right. I knew it even before he said it. I had known for some time, and if no one had had the courage to shoot me down, I may never have turned back. This was the crisis point I spoke about in the chapter on "Ego," and it was from this point on that I had a lot of unlearning to do and a lot of credibility to build back, especially with myself. While everyone else was showering me with praise, Vic knew that all I'd done was reach a level where I could fool your average listener, but he could see clear as day through the trick I was playing, and he knew that I would go no further than this trick as long as it worked for me. So he made a choice to shatter my illusion like glass rather than risk me settling for a lie that "worked." He didn't do it because he was cruel; he did it because he cared, and I believed him when he told me that he was invested in my journey. He was right. I wanted to become someone who communicated well, not for my own aggrandisement but to make a difference, and without this correction, I may never have gotten back on track.

What he said still stung, but I will be forever grateful that he rescued me.

❦

We all need honest mirrors to help us objectively see what and how we're really doing.

As human beings, we are hard-wired to look at the responses we generate from those around us to gauge our effect on, and standing with, others. We read faces in conversations, we read body language when dating, we read the tone of voice in interactions, all to glean how we are being received. So it should come as no surprise to us that we also eagerly look for signs of how our creative endeavours are perceived when we release them into the world.

There's nothing wrong with this, of course, but we have to remember that not all feedback is created equally, and it's a mistake to think that all critique should be given credence.

We spoke earlier about the fact that human beings use language in one of two ways: the first is to speak the Truth, and the second is to elicit a desired response. That's why it's especially challenging to find those honest mirrors in our lives. We have to sidestep the voices of those who are just feeding us compliments because of their own need to be liked. We must circumnavigate the voices of those trying to discourage us because of their own unacknowledged frustrations. Finding the precious Truth-speakers who will give us a good idea of how we're doing can be a very hard task, especially amidst all the noise.

We live in an age in which people are obsessed with their own opinions. Many feel entitled to give them constantly, whether or not anyone asked. Most people also have an expectation that their proffered opinions should be treated as sacred, and even perhaps that the rest of us should feel honoured in receiving them.

If we make things and share them with others, we have to be prepared for people to freely let us know how they feel about what we've done, whether we requested their input or not. If we're not able to put all those conflicting opinions in perspective, we may be faced with a confusing cacophony that leaves us baffled as to whether we've produced work we can be proud of or work we should be embarrassed by. We have to ground ourselves in that healthy self-centredness we talked about. We also have to get very particular in choosing which critiques are helpful and learn to turn the volume down on the general noise.

Nowhere is this more necessary than on the Internet and social media. Unfortunately, online spaces tend to collectively surface some of the worst in us as human beings, perhaps because we don't feel accountable for the things we say when hidden behind a veil of anonymity. We've all experienced at some point how comments sections and forums can be treacherous places filled with bile and vitriol, and the sooner we learn not to put stock in the opinions of angsty keyboard warriors, the better.

Here's something I've noticed: I've never encountered a talented online troll. I'm going to wager that you haven't, either. I'll guess that you've never received an unkind comment on something you've shared, clicked through to see what sort of work the commenter does, and just been shocked by the outstanding quality of their output. I think it's fairly obvious why: people who are good at what they do don't have time to go around leaving negative comments about other people's creativity. They are wrapped up in the "doing" themselves. Good artists don't troll. That means that most negativity comes from frustrated fellow creatives who haven't yet managed to produce work that they are proud of, so rather than put in the mountain of effort required to develop themselves, they decide to turn to the much less taxing game of pulling other people down in a vain attempt to level the playing field.

These people are easy to spot. Their comments are invariably negative. They lack nuance, empathy, or any sort of intelligent commentary. They show little compassion or genuine interest in what you're trying to do. They are brash and attention-seeking, often just rude for rudeness' sake. There are no useful suggestions for change, just words designed to make you feel bad about what you've made—and many of us tolerate this negativity because we've come to expect it on the Internet. However, we would never put up with it in real life.

Imagine this scenario.

You are sitting in a coffee shop when someone walks in and declares in a loud voice, "The decor in here is awful, the coffee is crap, and that barista has some of the worst facial hair I've ever seen!" After a stunned silence the owner would probably have to ask them to step outside to have a private chat with them about their complaints.

Imagine the customer then chooses to escalate things by yelling, "What, you can't take criticism? I'm sharing my opinion! Don't open a coffee shop if you can't take people telling you how terrible your coffee or your facial hair is!"

At this point, the coffee shop would have become a keenly uncomfortable space to be in because it's clear there is a very unstable person present. In fact, it's likely at this point that the police would be called.

It's no mystery what's going on when things like this happen in our real world. We all understand that this outburst and rudeness can't be about "decor," or "coffee," or "facial hair." This person is going through something, and their lack of emotional intelligence leaves them lashing out at peripheral things in acts of misguided venting. We also know that often this sort of behaviour is a cry for help or a bid for attention because someone is feeling desperately unseen. However sad we may feel for that person, though, we know that giving them the attention they crave as a reward for that behaviour will only reinforce it and guarantee it happens again.

In real life, we know not to take opinions offered like this seriously, but for some reason, we seem more tempted to absorb them when they are offered online, especially toward our own work. Perhaps it's because we can't see the face or read the tone of voice, but in any case, we need to learn to turn down the volume on these voices if we intend to share our work with the world.

Personally, I have absolutely no compunction about using the Block button on any of my online platforms if people don't approach politely, offering intelligent conversation, especially if the comment is critical. I apply the same rules online as I do in real life. I will give you all the time in the world if you approach to start a civil conversation. In fact, even if you have something negative to say, I will probably feel very flattered that you want to take the time to talk about something I've made. However, if you come knocking on the real front door of my real house, wearing a mask to protect your identity, only to vomit negativity on me and bluntly tell me that my work sucks, I obviously won't be inviting you in for tea.

Make no mistake: you will have to deal with this sort of thing at some point if you share your work with the world online. I think the best way to handle interactions like this is to think about who we might be interacting with. It's almost always an angry and thwarted fellow "maker of things" who just can't seem to find a way forward. In many cases, they have tried and failed, and they are worried they may never be able to produce anything that completes that artistic cycle and is appreciated by another human being, so they want to give up. Their mean words and pointed criticisms are far more about their own anger and fear than about your work. They actually deserve our unpatronising pity, not our anger.

Going further, I sometimes try to picture the specific individual on the other end. Is it a teenager living in a troubled home, unsure of how to deal with their own anger and frustration? Might they even be struggling with mental illness? If that's the case, then stepping up to them to fight back could amount to intellectual bullying, and I don't want to be that human being.

I admittedly often fail to live up to my own advice, but here it is nonetheless: don't engage. Remember where this criticism likely comes from, and tune it out. If you start to take it seriously, it could cripple your motivation and self-worth.

That goes for compliments, too, by the way. You may have begun to share your work and received a flood of congratulations, and you can feel your head beginning to swell with pride. As important as it is to ignore the anonymous negative commentary around your work, you should also keep a level head about the flippantly positive commentary that comes your way. Even though it feels great to receive and likely comes from people who genuinely wish you well and enjoy your work, it can tempt you to think you're better than you are and throw your Ego out of whack if you take it too seriously.

That's not to say we should ignore all anonymous or unsolicited critique. While it's dangerous to take onboard every criticism that comes our way and important to discern where it really comes from, we can't close ourselves off from outside critique altogether because we could end up missing useful information.

Trust yourself. You'll know a genuinely constructive critique when you hear it because it has a different tone. It's polite and respectful. It has useful information in it or suggestions for change, and it has some humility in its tone, especially if you didn't request feedback in the first place. Proper constructive criticism is always a good thing and sometimes will appear from unknown sources, so don't miss it or mistake it for something else, because that feedback can be gold. We just need to be discerning. Assessing motives will help us weed out the destructive and discouraging commentary, and self-awareness will prevent us from discounting the truly constructive critiques. If we're not able to hear constructive criticism at all, though, we hamstring our own growth and do ourselves a disservice.

I'm especially selective about the ongoing feedback I take seriously. There are only a small number of people whose opinion of my work I take to heart on a regular basis. It doesn't matter whether the content is positive or negative; for me to accept ongoing critique from someone, they have to pass one of two tests in my mind:

Does this person know what they're talking about?

Does this person really care?

Let's start with that first one: does this person really know what they're talking about?

One of the biggest reasons I won't take general criticism or praise to heart is that I want to know where it's coming from first, and that's often hard to tell, especially online. There's often no real name attached to the comment, and it's very hard to find their work, so I have no idea what expertise the commenter in question has. If I indiscriminately take on board all feedback, I will end up completely confused about what I'm doing; instead, I pay close attention to comments coming from people who clearly know what they're talking about. On the occasions I have let my guard down and absorbed negative criticism online, it's been because the person speaking has used their real name, and when I have gone to check out their work, I can see straightaway that they know their stuff.

That's important. It's the difference between firsthand and secondhand knowledge. Often you're getting feedback from someone telling you that you're "doing it wrong," but you can see that their work is still in its infancy and they haven't yet figured out how to apply the advice to their own output. In those cases, it's probably a mistake to dwell on their opinions because they are most likely just parroting back something they heard another artist say, rather than sharing their own experience born of blood, sweat, and tears. They didn't earn the knowledge and so it should be taken with a pinch of salt.

It would be like a first-year acting student contacting Tom Hanks to let him know that the work he did on his latest film wasn't up to scratch. I imagine that Tom would ignore the comment, or he may choose to engage graciously, but at no point would he make career-altering decisions based on the self-assured comments of a mouthy beginner. However, if Sir Anthony Hopkins got on the phone to give Tom notes on his latest film, I imagine that Tom would take that call. The difference is the expertise and skill of the individual offering the critique. Tom still might not take the advice, nor make the suggested changes because he is necessarily self-centred about his process, but he will almost certainly listen.

The commenter doesn't necessarily have to be engaged in the art form themselves, but at a minimum, they should be well-informed for you to take them seriously. This is why there is such a thing as "professional artistic criticism." Food critics, or film critics, or art critics spend years studying the arena they are commenting in. They are deeply knowledgeable. In some cases, critics have deliberately chosen not to engage directly in the art form themselves so that they can't be accused of professionally maligning their competition, and this positions them well to comment without being accused of having nefarious motives. It gives their critique credibility. It's the difference between a professional movie critic panning the last *Avengers* movie as "poorly constructed" and Martin Scorsese recently saying the franchise is "not real cinema." As great a filmmaker as Scorsese is and as much as we respect his work, those comments created a stir because they sounded to some like the words of a jealous fellow filmmaker annoyed that tickets sell better to Marvel movies than his own.

Professional critics have a role to play. They are experts in their field and have a historical knowledge of their subject matter across its various genres, and they hopefully pass judgement on work based on an unbiased and expert view. The best critics are fair, articulate, and well-respected, often even by those they are critiquing.

More than providing their targeted opinion to the artist in question, a good critic will actually teach the rest of us about the art form in general, and this can be a valuable learning tool when making our way up the ranks. For example, I'm a big fan of the *MasterChef: The Professionals* series, and one of my favourite rounds is when the contestants cook for the critics. Listening to their take on the food they are presented with is eye-opening because you can see them internally referencing the thousands of meals they've eaten in some of the best restaurants in the world and comparing the artistry of the plate in front of them with that extensive catalogue. I find that listening to their critiques helps me appreciate what it really takes to make a great plate of food.

In a similar vein, I'm a big fan of film critic Mark Kermode. I've listened to the various podcasts he has done for over 10 years now and read a couple of his books, and in doing so, I have learnt how to watch and appreciate films. I know more about the history of filmmaking. I understand references that the best filmmakers bury in their movies as nods to the past. I can better appreciate story structure, what a well-formed character looks like, what a "tight" or a "flabby" script sounds like—and thanks to listening to his take on the blockbusters of the last decade, I am no longer fooled by "spectacle." I need substance in my films. I've been educated about filmmaking by someone who has never made a film in his life, and that's possible because he has so thoroughly immersed himself in the world he comments on. If I were a filmmaker, I'd be foolish to simply dismiss his take on one of my films.

You may never experience the privilege of having a professional critic comment on your work. I've never had a professional critic comment on my work either, but I have learnt that when compliments or critique come from informed individuals, their opinion should be taken seriously.

In the chapter on "Logos," I told you the story of some criticism I received about the portraits I had made of the Himba tribe. The creative director of the print house told me that, as technically good as they may have been, they didn't speak to him at all, and he didn't care about them. If that comment had come from an anonymous stranger, perhaps I would have just dismissed it, but I didn't because it came from an expert in his field. He may not have been a photographer himself, but he prints exhibitions for some of the best photographers in the world, so he knows what he's talking about, and I would have been a fool not to take his critique onboard, chew it over, and work out what I could learn from it about my own work.

Just because most of us aren't at the level where we can expect professional critics to be coming around to look at our work doesn't mean we can't request it. We can seek out people who have deep knowledge of our chosen art form. We could book sessions with galleries who will give us time and feedback on our work. We could arrange professional portfolio reviews with artists or agencies who are willing to give some guidance based on their experience. Many artists now offer remote online review sessions where you can buy an hour of their time and receive detailed feedback on your work and suggestions for a way forward. One way to start is to identify those artists or institutions you really respect and see if any of them offer the opportunity—paid or for free—to get some expert eyes on your work.

You should always listen to expertise, with one caveat: be sure to assess the intention of the expert offering you feedback, especially if you didn't ask for it. You may find yourself in a situation in which someone further down the road than you is constantly commenting—and suspiciously willing and ready to tell you where you're missing the mark.

My friend Jeffery Saddoris, who has produced photography podcasts of one form or another for years, coined the phrase, "Beware the middle-management photographers." They are inarguably skilled and experienced, but they aren't at the top of the game yet and they seem obsessed with telling all those coming up behind them that they're doing it all wrong. They fixate on labels and categorizing everyone else's work into neat boxes. They are quick to suggest that their methods are the best and anyone doing it differently is "cheapening" photography. The worst of them even try turning other photographers' chosen processes into moral issues and accuse those who do things differently of bastardizing the art form.

I've had "middle-management photographers" tell me things like:

"Photoshop is evil."

"Film is the only pure form of photography."

"Your work doesn't fit in the category of street photography. You're not part of the club."

"Naturally lit portraits are the real thing because you have to learn to use available light."

"Studio strobe-lit portraits are far purer because you are responsible for building the light on your subject from scratch."

Those last two completely contradictory comments came from two different photographers—both vastly more experienced than I was—within the same week. Obviously, this left me more than a little confused.

You will meet people who have gone ahead of you and have a great deal more experience than you, but that doesn't mean their opinion should automatically be taken as gospel. They may be frustrated at their own lack of success and threatened by the talented individuals they see climbing up after them. Sometimes, their speeches about the right and wrong way to do things are simply justifications for their own methods and an attempt to denounce anything new, especially if it threatens their position. These attempts to limit you are, again, just uncalibrated Egos who are threatened by your progress and frustrated with their own stagnation. To take it seriously is to hamstring your own journey. Admittedly, it would be tempting to use this as a convenient excuse to dismiss all critique from the old guard that we don't like, but that would be an equally egregious mistake.

So how do we separate the wheat from the chaff and work out which critique is valuable?

&

Everyone cares about something, and every critique, unless asked for, is offered for a reason. It might be because the person offering the feedback cares about protecting their patch and putting you off, or it might be because they care about you and want to see you realise your potential. Discerning those motives is important.

As Theodore Roosevelt said, "No one cares how much you know until they know how much you care."

Back in my mid-20s, I had a weekly dinner appointment with my friend Doug. We would pick a restaurant—usually something cheap because we were both students at the time—and settle in for a good few hours of conversation. The rule on those evenings was that no topic was off the table, and we would hold nothing back. Free-flowing honesty was the deal we made with each other.

Early on in our friendship, we'd recognised in each other conscientious young men who were earnest about growing into the best version of ourselves we possibly could. So we decided to collaborate in that endeavour. When you're at that stage of your life, you are desperate to get a good read on how you're doing, and so we decided to act as mirrors for each other.

Sitting down at the table, we would order some food and then share how our week had gone—things that had happened, conversations we'd had—and the agreement was to do this as honestly as we could manage. So much of the way we recount our life experiences with others is pushed through a filter designed to maximise both our heroic deeds and the injustices done to us by others because, again, too often we use language to elicit a favourable response rather than to tell the Truth. Doug and I agreed, though, to be aware of when we were offering anything less than complete honesty and to always choose to be harsher on ourselves than on others in the telling of our stories. We weren't trying to impress each other; we were attempting to be vulnerable about our flaws so we could root them out and choose differently in the future, and to do that well we couldn't hold anything back.

As church-going young men at the time, we used a verse from one of the wisdom books in the Bible as our statement of intent. "As iron sharpens iron, so one person sharpens another" (Proverbs 27:17).

Not only did we have to be honest about our own flaws, but we also had to give our honest critique of what we saw in each other's choice of words and actions over the past week. It was our duty to probe each other's decisions and thinking, and to call out when we thought the other could have done better. It is always tempting to make excuses for our actions and explain things away, but we never did. We listened. We took in what was being said. I'm sure I gave and received harsher criticisms over those dinners with my friend than I have done with anyone else before or since, yet I never once left feeling bad. Just the opposite. No matter how critical Doug had been on any given night, I felt seen, understood, and even cared for.

Why?

I knew Doug's intention. I had no doubt that he genuinely cared about me. He honestly could have said anything to me because it was always clear where that criticism came from, and what its purpose was.

One key reason that criticism stings is that we suspect it comes with an attack behind it—and we're often not wrong. When it does, we need to be on guard. But the minute we realise that it comes from a place of genuine concern and care, things change immediately.

Doug and I had a pact and for that pact to work we both had to be simultaneously ruthless and compassionate in our honesty. It's a hard balance to strike, but I learnt that you can say almost anything if you make sure that you've communicated how much you care first, not to soften the blow but to state your intentions so your critique makes its way through the walls that reflexively get thrown up within all of us. Not once was I hurt by Doug's critiques because I knew my friend wanted the best for me.

I believe that we learn much more about ourselves from critical feedback than we do from positive feedback, so it's really important to listen to the voices of those we trust, who care about us, and whom we will always be willing to hear no matter how close to the bone their comments cut. We won't develop well as artists, or as human beings, unless we build a few of those "honest mirrors" into our lives.

&

I would suggest there are three mirrors we need to find.

The first mirror is an artist you can journey alongside.

You need to find your "Doug."

Remember you don't have to be a professional to offer feedback. You aren't setting yourself up as an experienced art critic; you're just offering to mirror what you see to someone you care about for the sole purpose of seeing them become the best creator they can possibly be. You don't even have to share in the same art form to build these sorts of relationships. Why can't a painter and a photographer meet over a table to talk about their work? Why not a writer and a musician? At the end of the day, it's just about saying what you see and supporting each other on your respective journeys.

You will have to commit to being open to their criticism without being offended or defensive. In setting up this sort of partnership, you are giving them permission to say anything they believe needs to be said in order to help you see your blind spots, no matter how tough it may sound. You have to provide your chosen travel companion with a sense of safety, trust, and freedom to say anything, because if you give them a justification, or an excuse, or an "annoyed" response, they will soon decide it's not worth being honest with you. You have to let them know you are ready and willing to hear what they have to say.

You also have to commit to being honest in your criticism of your partner. This is especially hard for those who fear conflict. Perhaps you aren't well-versed in saying things that could prompt a defensive reaction, but this relationship doesn't work unless you risk displeasing the person sitting across the table from you. The honesty you offer will be the honesty you receive. You have to match each other and even try and outdo each other in how incisive and pointed you can be with your critique, all the while showing how much you care about your partner becoming the very best version of themselves.

Look around you. Find someone you think you could journey with and offer to meet regularly to talk about your work and what you're trying to accomplish. Show each other what you're working on. Set goals that you hold each other accountable for hitting. Build a genuine connection of care between you. I would hazard a guess that this individual will soon become very precious to you as you invest in each other's journeys and get to know each other deeper than many human beings do.

The second mirror is a mentor.

You need to find your "Vic."

This is the Holy Grail of good critique because great mentors are both experienced and knowledgeable about their art form, and the good ones are also unthreatened, nurturing, and willing to help you develop and benefit from their experience. They will share what they've learnt over their own journey and will genuinely care about helping you find your voice and becoming the best version of yourself.

I'll acknowledge that it's very hard to find good mentors these days. I get the feeling it used to be easier when we had systems of apprenticeship in the Middle Ages, and even into the industrial era, but it seems our digital age has separated us more than ever. A competitive spirit has crept into the hearts of many, leaving them unwilling to help others for fear of creating competition.

So what can you do?

Start with identifying someone whose work you respect. Again, they don't necessarily have to be directly engaged in your art form. You may find that you benefit hugely from their life experience and vision alone, and that you can teach yourself the techniques you need on your own steam. Either way, you are looking for someone whose work you respect and whom you admire as a person. A mentor will often shape your view of the world, so before you climb into the mould, make sure you like the shape.

When it's time to approach them and ask if they would be willing to help you, don't just walk in and ask for their time. Find ways to add value to their work first. Get creative. Come up with some sort of exchange.

If they're a painter, offer to come in once a week and help them organise their space in exchange for casting an eye over some of your latest pieces to see what they see.

If they're a photographer, offer to help organise their images into cohesive and keyworded catalogues on their hard drives in exchange for giving you some feedback on your latest images.

In short, you're looking for ways you can add value before you ask for value to be added for you.

A word of warning: make sure that you aren't choosing your mentor just to steal from their work. It's too easy to choose someone we want to imitate and lazily copy and paste their techniques, but we will do ourselves a disservice by not allowing our own voice to emerge, and we will soon lose the trust of our chosen mentor as we reveal ourselves to be an "artistic spy." Be hard on yourself about developing your own voice, and at all costs resist the temptation to vampirically milk their hard-earned knowledge to get ahead.

Your motivation is going to be crucial. You should be asking a mentor to give you their opinion on the work you are producing in your own authentic voice and requesting ideas about what to explore going forward. A good mentor won't try and force you into their style. Instead, they will push you to create something new and unique to you.

Some mentors may be reluctant at first, but if you prove your value to them, if you are grateful for the critique they give you, and you show diligent work and progress, I would imagine that nothing in the world will be able to keep them from caring deeply about you and your journey.

The third mirror is you.

If we find ourselves developing our skills, we need to turn around and find someone else to mentor. We forget this step because most of us are just trying to get ahead ourselves, and we are constantly gazing up the ladder at how far we have to go, paying little attention to those coming up behind us. Just imagine, though, how much it would have meant to us if someone we respected had approached us when we were just getting started and offered to help. It would have meant the world, and you could offer that to someone else.

Maybe you're reading this, and you are that experienced professional. Maybe you're even retired with more time on your hands and a truckload of skills to share. My challenge to you is to find someone to mentor. Tell them how it works and what you are willing to do for them. Explain how they will need a "tough skin" if they accept, but promise that your motivation will always be to see them reach their potential because you care about their journey. If we all took this proactive third step, it would no longer be such a challenge to find a good mentor.

We all need critique, but not all critique is helpful, so get selective. Turn down the volume on the general noise your work creates. Remember to stay open and receptive to constructive criticism, even if it's difficult to hear. Don't forget that the most accurate constructive criticism will be painful, so employ some emotional intelligence when you get defensive because there might be something to learn in there.

The pain is how we know it's true. Learn from it, and even be big enough to thank your constructive critic for caring enough to offer it.

Then organise those professional critique sessions, build those creative friendships, find that mentor, and pass it on by offering to mentor someone else.

We all need those mirrors that tell us the Truth.

Feel

Of all the jobs I've done in my adult life, there is one that I found especially fulfilling. When I was studying at the seminary, I needed to get extra work to pay the rent, so I picked up a part-time job as an aftercare teacher. When my lectures finished for the day, I would race across to the local primary school just as they were letting out from their classes, and it was then my job to sit and do homework with the children for the afternoon until their parents could pick them up.

I had a deal with my class of 30 or so that once they had all completed their homework, I would take them out to the sports fields for some games. One day it might be cricket, the next maybe soccer, and on hot days things had a habit of just descending into a water fight.

The teachers among you will know that there are always some children who stand out to you as needing a little more attention and help, and those are the ones who quickly worm their way into your heart. In my case, there was one boy of about 10 years old in my class who was going through a particularly rough time at home. His parents were getting a divorce, and they seemed to be asking him to make the decision about whom he wanted to live with, which was tearing him apart. It seemed to me inordinately unfair to put such a hefty decision on such a young mind.

It was often the case that whilst the other kids were running around the sports fields in the late afternoon sun, I would take a break and sit on the grassy bank, and this young man would come and sit beside me.

Some days he wanted to talk and tell me what was going on.

Some days we spoke about movies or computer games because it seemed he just wanted a distraction.

Some days I offered him what little comfort I could.

Some days we just watched the other kids running around and enjoyed the sight of the setting sun.

I felt powerless to help him but happy to be there for him in whatever ways he needed.

One day he met me at the gates of the school, and as I walked up, he handed me a painting. In it two stick figures stood in a field of green, the sky afire with the colours of an improbably vivid sunset. He briefly and bashfully explained that in class that day they had been given the task of making a painting around the theme of "friendship." He told me he had decided to paint the two of us talking beside the sports fields as we often did in the afternoons.

I'll be honest; the painting was a technical horror show. No detail in the huge, sweeping brush strokes. No perspective control, with the stick figures appearing pretty much the same size as the trees. Bits of white paper showing through where he had missed spots, and colours running into other colours where he hadn't. Even the paper was heavily wrinkled from being oversaturated by watercolour paints and then allowed to dry too fast. However, I have had the privilege of standing in front of original works by Vermeer, Rembrandt, van Gogh, and Rubens, and none have come close to moving me the way that painting did. This artistic train wreck would win no awards, but it was one of the most beautiful things I had ever seen.

This young man had never said "thank you" out loud for the time we had spent talking or for my support, and I would have never expected him to, but this piece he had made screamed how much that time had meant to him. It conveyed his feelings beyond words, and it moved me deeply in return. That painting lived on my fridge door at home for many years until it was regrettably lost in a move. As art goes, it was one of the most affecting pieces I have ever laid eyes on.

The things we make have the power to convey emotion. They can communicate what we feel to others, and in turn, we can elicit feelings in the people who experience the things we've made. Getting a handle on this potential and using it more deliberately may help us make more meaningful things, and learning the balance between using our emotions as a guide and not being self-indulgent with them can help us better formulate what we want to communicate in our work.

⁊

We tend to create a false dichotomy around the idea of emotions. You'll hear many people say things like, "There are two kinds of people in this world: ones who make their decisions emotionally and ones who make their decisions rationally." Many personality tests seek to categorise us as either "thinking" or "feeling" types, which only serves to reinforce this dualistic notion. A good number of those personality tests work off Carl Jung's ideas around our emotions and our rational minds, but I don't think his intention in suggesting these distinctions was to help us neatly categorise ourselves as one or the other, putting ourselves in the right conceptual box, or metaphorically sticking the right label onto our foreheads. We were never meant to resign ourselves to the idea that we represent only one side of that coin.

All human psyches are made up of a mix of both rational and emotional. We all think and we all feel, and if we want to be better-integrated individuals and better-rounded artists, the trick is to identify which realm we operate in more intuitively and make an effort to incorporate more of our weaker side and balance ourselves out.

Artists, in particular, have to ride a difficult line between their intellects and their emotions. Too much feeling-based work and we can get self-indulgent and lost, but on the other side, too much thinking-based work and we may play it too safe and lose emotional impact. We must make the effort both to formulate and conceptualise what we're doing and to put our heart into it. The "thinking" and the "feeling" need to work in harmony.

&

On one side of the coin, we need our rational minds to help direct our acts of creation.

It's our rational minds that help us construct what we want to say with our work as we make decisions about the things we care about and plan out our projects to make sure that the message we are putting across is the one we intend.

It's our rational minds that help us systematically learn the skills of our chosen art form. We rationally choose where and how to teach ourselves, whether through our selection of influences or the courses we take or the artistic partnerships we form. We then store all the tricks of the trade we've learnt in our rational minds, ready to unleash them the moment the muse strikes.

It's our rational minds that help us determine our long-term direction, to envision where we would like our work to be in 10 years, and to come up with the necessary plans to get there.

Our rational minds also stop us from getting too self-indulgent with our work and help us to find ways to make it more relatable. If our work came only out of our feelings with no effort made to translate those feelings for others, we may find that what we make is too specific to us, too niche, dare I say "too self-absorbed." In order for art to serve as effective communication, for our creations to "land well" with our audience, we have to offer some sense of understanding of and empathy for those who will experience our work.

There is also a danger to artists themselves in delving too deeply into their emotional worlds to the exclusion of all else. The stereotype of the "troubled artist" is an old one and one I fear too many see as a romantic ideal without taking stock of the damage it's done to many. There is a voluminous tome to be written recounting the real-life addictions, ruined relationships, and lost lives of artists who felt they needed to give themselves over to their emotions with reckless abandon.

Our work will often ask us to visit our own darkness from time to time and to look it in the face, but if we stare too long, like Sméagol's obsessing over the One Ring, we will be lost to ourselves and those who love us. In fact, the corrupting, mesmeric MacGuffin of many a movie plot is a well-worn trope for a reason: human beings recognised this particular danger a long time ago, and we've woven warnings into the fabric of our stories.

Our rational minds are the foil that serves to balance those tendencies. They allow us to go deep but stay tethered to something truer and more stable than our shifting moods. They allow us to make our way far into the maze, knowing that we still have a thread to follow back into the light when we are done.

For artists, tying our motivation to our feelings is also a risk. If we "make" based only on our moods, then the impetus to make will change as often as our moods do, and we may find ourselves creating a confusing mess—if we end up making at all. I hear too many artists say things like, "I didn't make anything this week because I just wasn't feeling it." For those of us with a tendency to allow our emotional ups and downs to direct us, it's important to try and relocate our drive to our rational minds.

There is this assumption among artists that inspiration is a feeling. "I feel inspired today" is something you hear a lot. I don't agree, though. I'm not sure we mean "inspired" when we identify that particular feeling. We may feel "motivated" or "excited" to make today, but as we've established, inspiration—true in-spiration, true in-breath—is something we work ourselves into, not something we feel. When we say we "feel uninspired," we usually mean that we are demotivated and running out of ideas. But we can rationally take steps toward in-spiration by changing our mindset and taking some practical actions.

We've already discussed how we need to make sure we fill our minds with new ideas through the things we consume— what we listen to, read, and watch—and then remember the importance of creating generative mental space if we want to be in-spired. But we can't make these efforts only when we feel like it. It would be hitching the cart of our motivation to the wild horses of our shifting emotions.

We don't "feel" our way into in-spiration; we "work" our way in.

How many times have you felt demotivated but forced your-self to pick up the camera or the paintbrush, or sit down at the typewriter anyway and then found yourself there hours later, still happily making? It just happened to me. I knew I had to sit down and write today, but I really didn't feel like it. However, I didn't allow my feelings to make the decision about whether I would write today. Instead, I let my rational mind choose. I told myself that even though I didn't feel like it, it was a good idea to try. So I made coffee, put on some ambient music, and started typing, and now I've been here for over an hour and have over 2,000 new words on the screen in front of me, including this last sentence. That start-ed with a rational choice I made that saw me go from doing nothing to making something and enjoying the process. But to get there, I had to override the sense that I didn't really feel like it. I'm grateful I did.

In-spiration doesn't strike as a feeling while you're sitting on the couch waiting for it. In-spiration most often strikes when you've already gotten yourself up and begun to create. On the hardest days, "making" has to begin with a rational choice.

It's about playing the long game too and making the de-cision to try as often as we can, especially when we don't feel like it. Some days I don't feel like taking photographs, but I go out anyway because it's a discipline I've chosen for myself. Some days I come home with nothing to show for it, and some days I come home with a good haul of images, but when I'm putting together my annual book of photography, I look back and I'm so grateful for all the times I used my rational mind to talk myself into picking up the camera, because there are now so many more images to choose from, which makes for a stronger book. More than that, it's clear that many of my favourite images from any given year were made on days when I had to force myself out the door—days when picking up the camera came down to a rational choice. Those images may never have happened if I had let my emotions run the show.

What's the worst thing that could happen by ignoring the "unmotivated" and "uninspired" feelings we all have from time to time and choosing to make something anyway? Personally, I can't think of a single time I've regretted that rational choice. This isn't to say that it's always worked out and I've made things I'm proud of every time I got off the couch, but even on those occasions when it hasn't panned out, I've never regretted trying. Don't wait until you "feel" it. Emotions are important, but they shouldn't be our primary driver. Create as often as you can choose to, even when you don't feel like it, even if it doesn't work out. Once again, you can't control the results, but you can control whether you get up and pick up the pen, the guitar, or the camera in an act of service to the Muses.

I don't want to sound insensitive to those out there who deal with genuine mood disorders. I've battled depression at various points in my life, so I understand, but even then I had choices, like whether to reach out to friends, or take myself for regular walks, or book an appointment with a professional to get help. There is always something you can do to move in a positive direction, even if all you can manage today is one tiny step.

As people who tend to be pretty connected to our emotions, artists may at times vilify the rational mind as a less creative part of our psyche, but making sure that we use it in combination with our emotions will make us better, more skilled, more deliberate, more consistent, more regularly in-spired creators.

&

On the other side of the coin, we need our feelings to make beautiful things.

I told you I played in a few bands in my twenties, but I didn't tell you that I led those bands as well. I would organise the practice sessions, choose what songs we put in our repertoire, book the gigs, put the setlists together, and direct the band from my keyboard as we played live. Even though we had the setlist for each night, there was no guarantee that the songs would be played in that order or that we would play them the same way each time. I liked to keep things as fluid as possible. When rehearsing, we split up the songs into sections and practiced how to move between verse, chorus, bridge, and interlude in any order in each song so that we had as many options as possible for every performance. We even prepared relative major and minor key versions of some of the songs that we could wheel out depending on the tone of the gig we were playing.

I had also developed a set of simple, subtle hand signals that I would give behind my back to the rest of the band to let them know where we were heading.

Two fingers down was a verse.

A cupped hand was a chorus.

A tapping finger was a build.

A flat hand was a breakdown.

A pointing finger to a specific band member meant we were going into an instrumental section featuring that musician, so the rest of us needed to drop back and support.

A swirling finger called to repeat the section we were on.

A closed fist brought the song to an end.

You get the idea.

Now, this was all rational mind stuff that had been prepared beforehand and allowed us to perform like this. Hours of practice, learning songs and sections, planning hand signals, and a foreknowledge of the sort of venue and crowd we were performing to all made up the information we needed.

However, during the performance, it was all about "feel." To make sure we had a good set, I needed to pay close attention to what I was feeling, what the rest of the band was feeling, and especially, what the collective room we were playing to was feeling. On many nights, even though I might have been looking into a crowd of 300 faces, it was more like trying to read the emotions on a single face and feel out where they wanted to go. In that, there was a "give and take." Some nights it was more about them, and even though we might not have been feeling it, we could tell they were, so we stayed with a particular section that the room was responding to. Other nights we could tell the crowd wasn't feeling it but we were as a band, so almost in defiance, we revelled in the joy of playing the music we loved and often won over the room that way.

We did all that rehearsing and had those hand signals to keep us together, but using them correctly had little to do with my rational mind. I had to feel out what was needed in the moment, and many gigs went in very different directions from the way I had imagined they would before we played the first note. If I had chosen to follow my rational mind and stick strictly to a prepared plan, I wouldn't have been able to course-correct on the fly, but paying attention to those unconscious senses led to some very special nights for us as musicians.

Truth be told, many times the hand signals weren't even necessary. I occasionally forgot to signal on time, yet we got to the point as a group where we could intuit in unison what would come next. Playing like that was an almost mystical experience. There is a near-telepathy that develops between band members who play together for years, where they synchronously know exactly what a moment requires and musically move in that direction together, like the murmuration of a flock of birds. I often used to wonder how that was possible. I remember talking about it as a band on a few occasions but we could never adequately explain it. Because we knew each other really well at this point, we could anticipate each other's playing, but the fact was that every gig and every crowd was different, so there were many more variables than just the five of us on stage. Every audience member was a variable too, and they set the tone and the direction for the night as much as we did. I think it is better explained through our collective emotional sensitivity.

&

I'm aware of how woo-woo this sounds. On the surface, I'm a slightly repressed and stuffy Brit with a culturally expected suspicion of big displays of emotion, so talking like this isn't personality-driven. I don't have a choice, though, because in my experience, it's the truth. Making meaningful things requires emotional intelligence and sensitivity.

How often have you felt stuck or stalled in your making? You're not sure where to go next or what to say. This feeling surfaces most often when we've just finished a project and we're looking for a fresh direction for the next.

Maybe you've finished a series of paintings and want to try a new style but have no idea where to begin.

Maybe you've finished writing a book and want to start another but have no idea what it should be about.

Maybe you're a photographer who's grown accustomed to shooting in a particular town in a particular way, but you've moved and the change in context means you will have to begin again, and you're not sure how to start rebuilding.

Well, the rational decision in these cases is to just start painting, or writing, or photographing, but of course, it will be confusing for a while because starting something new almost always begins in Chaos. This is where our feelings are essential. They will be the guiding hand through the darkness as we try new techniques or approach new subjects. We can often feel when we're on the right track long before we can articulate why we know that, and in my experience, it is worth trusting that feeling when it surfaces.

What we're really talking about here is intuition. That "on the right track" feeling is our subconscious instinct bypassing our conscious rational mind to give us a thousand "yes" and a thousand "no" signals as we fumble our way forward. The more we do something, the more we will learn to trust our feelings around it because they inevitably lead to breakthroughs if we stick with them.

Some of us struggle because we lean too hard and rely too much on our rational minds. I'm one of them. I have a need to understand, control, and define, which often holds me back in the things I make. I've fallen into the trap of trying to neatly conceptualise every instinct before I allow myself to act on it, which I think comes from a fear of failure or making a fool of myself. The result is that I move much slower than I need to. I've had to teach myself that not every decision I make needs to make neat sense and that sometimes a gut feeling is the only way forward.

For example, there was a good while where I wouldn't let myself take a photograph unless the composition adhered to a traditionally accepted rule or formula, or featured a clear subject people would understand. All the elements had to be in place before I gave myself permission to click the shutter. I was my own bullying, dictatorial boss who insisted I had a succinct answer before I took a single creative action, and for a long time, it stifled my growth as a photographer.

I clearly remember the day I became aware of how ridiculous I was being. What did I think I was protecting myself from? What was the fear I was slavishly serving? Perhaps if I shot on film, I could argue that every image cost money to develop so I needed to be frugal, but there are no costs associated with filling a digital memory card with images. I certainly couldn't argue that I would be embarrassed when the world saw my photographic experimentations, because I could simply make the choice not to show anyone if the images didn't work out. Again, I had to go to war with my perfectionism and my need for control in order to give myself the freedom to play again and feel my way toward new things.

So now, when I walk around, I take a lot of images. I allow myself to photograph things by instinct. If I round a corner and just sense that something is there but I'm not consciously sure of what it is, I will give myself permission to visually explore with my camera by moving around and shooting loosely to see what reveals itself.

I will take an image. Look at it. Pay attention to how it feels. I'll then move position and change the angle, then take another image, and repeat this process a few times, asking myself, "Does that feel better, or worse?" It almost becomes a game of "warmer, cooler" with my feelings, which leads me toward something good. Most of the images I take to arrive at the good shot are admittedly junk, but I've owned that as part of the process. I used to be concerned with my "hit rate," which is something photographers often obsess about. It describes the number of "keepers" you take in a given day versus the number of images it took you to get there in total. Some would suggest that the lower that ratio is, the better photographer you are. Now, however, I would suggest that if you're playing that game in your head, you might be in danger of "making" too much out of your rational mind and not enough from your emotional gut.

I now make a point of sharing many of those intuitive experiments online. I call them "visual notes," and they are images I would never print and hang on a wall, nor put in a portfolio, but the act of taking them taught me something new, and I want to remember it. My Instagram at the moment is a scrapbook of ideas, rather than a portfolio designed to impress, because I want it to be a loose visual notebook for me and a vulnerably offered teaching tool for others so they can see more of the inside process that helps me arrive at the good stuff.

As I feel my way forward through experimentation, new avenues and visual styles have opened up to me in ways that wouldn't have been possible had I forced myself to pass them through the unforgiving sieve of my rational mind. Those "visual notes" are often the images that hold the breakthroughs to something new. Allowing myself to make things intuitively without a need for neat answers about "why" is progress for a perfectionist like me.

If you feel stuck, it might be worth doing things differently to get out of your rational head and feel your way forward.

I know a veteran architect who turns his initial sketches for buildings upside down and back to front to see how the building feels as a shape when it's disoriented.

Similarly, I have a photographer friend who does his dodging and burning work with the image placed upside down so that he is looking only at light and shape without the context of the final image, and he says it helps him intuitively achieve a better balance.

In the documentary *The Bee Gees: How Can You Mend a Broken Heart*, Chris Martin of Coldplay explains that Barry Gibb once showed him his guitar tuning. Martin says he didn't understand it, but he thought that Gibb made it complicated on purpose because "having no idea what you're doing on the guitar leads to you just hearing if you like it, rather than thinking if you like it." Gibb found a way to stumble into new sounds and chord structures because he moved beyond the narrow confines of the conventional.

Emotions are a guide, especially when we don't have any intellectual idea about how to move forward, but we do have a sense. "I'm not sure why, but . . . "

". . . I feel like this piece needs more blue."

". . . I feel like we should move to an A minor from here."

". . . I feel like this photo essay should be entirely in black-and-white."

Don't rationalise it yet. Act on that gut feeling, experiment around it, and see where it goes. We have to be able to give ourselves permission to follow these inclinations without having to tidily formulate the "why" before we make a move. Maybe we'll find out that it was a mistake to head down that particular road, but at least we listened, tried to follow our gut, and learned something in the process.

&

To use our emotions in a healthy way requires self-aware-ness. If we choose not only to be led intuitively by our feelings but also to find the content of what we want to say in our own emotions, then we need to be aware of what they are really telling us.

Art that flows from the emotions of a person who hasn't yet found self-awareness doesn't have the same integrity to it. There is a huge difference, for example, between an adolescent, anti-establishment young rocker yelling his fury onstage when his life has lacked any real struggle and the anti-establishment fire and passion of a speech given by Martin Luther King, Jr. The former is likely "assumed" emotion for the sake of artistic identity and won't last because it doesn't come from an authentic story. But the latter has weight because it comes from a human being who lived that pain, experienced that injustice, and worked through his own feelings before choosing how to communicate that righteous anger to the world in a way that landed and changed things.

Art that comes from true self-awareness connects with us on a deeper level.

Let's take Edvard Munch reproducing his inner turmoil in his painting entitled *The Scream*. Discussing the inspiration behind this piece, he said:

I was walking along the road with two friends—the sun was setting—suddenly the sky turned blood red—I paused, feeling exhausted, and leaned on the fence—there was blood and tongues of fire above the blue-black fjord and the city—my

friends walked on, and I stood there trembling with anxiety—
and I sensed an infinite scream passing through nature.

His description is full of emotion, and through it, he fully owns his personal struggle with anxiety. He doesn't try to hide it behind other emotions like anger or sorrow as many do; instead, he lets the unfiltered feeling he experienced that day flow out through paint and pastels onto the canvas, with no apparent fear of how it would make him look. It's that bold and courageous sharing of his authentic emotional state that moves viewers so deeply and leaves them lingering a little longer before moving on to other works in the gallery.

I believe that this image is as famous as it is in part because anxiety is such a common malady in our modern world. So many look upon this painting and relate profoundly to the feelings it evokes because it illustrates their own often non-sensical terror and the unbidden desire to scream, which surfaces in them daily.

Munch's courage in owning his emotional struggle and choosing to share it with the world as it was, unvarnished and unsanitised, brings strange comfort to many, who view it knowing that there are others out there who suffer as they do.

As discussed in the chapter on "Envy," our emotions are al-ways pointing to something in us that needs our attention, and applying emotional intelligence to that emotion can help us uncover what that something is. If we take the inner jour-ney to discover what that feeling in us really means, beyond first assumptions, and we choose to bravely travel that road to its redemptive conclusion by facing our fears, we stand a chance of making the good and necessary changes our subconscious is clamouring for. We'll then find that those same emotions no longer hold the same confusion or dread when they reoccur, which means that we can create out of those emotional spaces and offer others the beneficial lessons of our inward journey.

Our emotions are only the subconscious signposts to something more important. Sticking with them without working out where they lead is as useless as becoming obsessed with a bright red stop sign on a journey of a thousand miles. The sign is there to help you reach your destination safely, not for you to stop the car and stall your journey. This is where we have to balance our felt emotions with our rational minds again to make sure we're not getting stuck at the signposts.

In the same way, our emotions aren't the end of our message, but rather they offer us direction toward the message in our work. Once we've taken the inward journey for ourselves and know where the road leads, we can effectively share those feelings with others to help in their journeys.

Think about that piece of music that makes you cry every time you hear it.

What about the film that, when you watch, always leaves you in tears?

How about that book that always brings you such comfort?

These artists are likely working hard to create out of their lived stories, and it's worth paying attention to how they translate their experience of life into the things they make and how they elicit that emotional response from you. They could help you in your own acts of creation and teach you how to put more pathos into the things you make yourself.

I am especially conscious of drawing from this deeper well when I am putting together a film I've made.

I use techniques to get viewers to feel things. You might be surprised to hear that the longest part of the editing process for me isn't cutting the timeline or grading the footage; it's choosing the right soundtrack. This often takes me hours—it has to be perfect. Music is an essential ingredient because I know well that nothing swells the emotions and leads people toward that thing I want them to feel like music does. On the flip side, nothing can break the spell of a film more than a misplaced piece of music, so the time I take to find that perfect piece is always well-spent.

Don't get me wrong: things like creating a particular colour grade, controlling the pacing of cuts, and even intonating my spoken words also contribute to imbuing what I'm saying in the film with a specific feeling. If I push a script I've written into an automated text-to-speech program and use that robotic voice in my films, we all know it would completely lose emotional impact. However, if I accompany that speech

I've written with the right on-screen visuals, the right pacing, the right delivery, and especially the right soundtrack, it suddenly becomes infinitely more emotionally powerful.

My goal isn't to manipulate, though. I'm hard on myself, always ensuring that I am talking about things I've experienced, and if I am attempting to spark an emotion in a viewer, it's never just to tug at the heartstrings for its own sake. If I am being deliberate about trying to get my viewers to feel something, it's always an emotion I have experienced myself, and again, I'm not interested in getting them to just onanistically sit and stare at the emotional signpost; I want them to take the journey. At some point, I have attempted the road myself and I'm coming back to share what I've learned and emotionally describe where it leads, all in the hope that people who view my work will choose to take those roads for themselves.

My hope is that honestly conveying my feelings and leading you to feel the same through something I've made might just open you up. It may help you to celebrate, or grieve, or give you resolve. It may help you face your own confusing feelings with more courage because you know others feel just as you do. It may help you decide to take the inward journey, work out what those emotions are pointing to, and change your life for the better by facing your fears.

Maybe, just maybe, if I get it right, I really could bring a little Order to someone's Chaos.

At the age of 16, William Ernest Henley had to have his left leg amputated because of complications after contracting tuberculosis. If that wasn't bad enough, years later he began to develop issues with his right leg and was told by doctors that he would need to have it removed as well.

He didn't give up, though, and decided to travel to Edinburgh, where a surgeon by the name of Joseph Lister agreed to apply his considerable skill and attempt to rescue Henley's right leg. The surgeries seemed to have worked, and as he recovered in his hospital bed, Henley felt moved to write the now-famous poem, "Invictus," which he published in 1888:

Out of the night that covers me
Black as the pit from pole to pole,
I thank whatever gods may be
For my unconquerable soul.

In the fell clutch of circumstance,
I have not winced nor cried aloud.
Under the bludgeonings of chance
My head is bloody, but unbowed.

Beyond this place of wrath and tears
Looms but the Horror of the shade,
And yet the menace of the years
Finds, and shall find, me unafraid.

It matters not how strait the gate,
How charged with punishments the scroll,
I am the master of my fate:
I am the captain of my soul.

Here is a man who didn't just stare at the signposts of his quiet natural fear and despair. He took the inward road and faced his emotional turmoil, and then he came back to put pen to paper, and syntax to his feelings in order to leave us with one of the most famous poems ever written—so famous, in fact, that these words would comfort an aging Nelson Mandela as he sat in prison over 100 years later, and reportedly even saw him reciting the poem to fellow prisoners to bring them comfort in their hardships.

This is art from one heart to another, conveying the feelings of one human being to another, bringing comfort and Order to our felt Chaos.

Shadows

I was a quietly angry, angsty young man in my twenties. A low-level broiling frustration always thrummed away under the hood. Like for many at this age, it usually took the form of a generalised frustration at all the apparent injustice in the world, but as righteous as my anger felt, I didn't understand it because I hadn't faced it head-on and asked myself what it was trying to tell me. So many of my efforts to change the world for the better ended up being misguided and ineffectual. In my mind, I was slaying dragons, but in reality, I was often just tilting at windmills.

I said earlier that you would hear about Vic again in this book. Now, I want to tell you the most profound thing he ever taught me.

One semester at seminary we had been asked to write a paper on the relevance of the institutional church in the modern era. Well, this was one I was locked and loaded to answer, and I couldn't wait to dive in.

My main role at the time was caring for youth and young adults, which typically meant anyone from ages 13 to 35. That meant that I would have input on their lives from early high school into their years at university. Working across this age range, I saw a recurring pattern emerge. Throughout their teenage years, they enjoyed church life and seemed to accept everything they were told without question, most likely to please their families or to fit into the community. However, when they returned home for their first holidays from university, they would often pull me aside, feeling a little betrayed that the church hadn't been honest with them. In their lectures, they had been exposed to exciting new ideas, many of which didn't fit with the things they had been told by some in the church. Their scientific explorations, in particular, had uncovered some of the more primitive notions that still exist in the minds of some church-goers, but they also started to meet people of different sexualities, spiritualities, and political standpoints from themselves and began to realise new things about humanity in general and in some cases, about themselves as well.

It infuriated me that the response from a lot of threatened church leaders to this influx of new questions and ideas was only to shoot them down or attempt to silence them. These were kids I cared about, and I couldn't have been more excited that their minds were aflame with new ideas. I had a reputation even back then of being honest about where the church fell short and where their ideas were outdated, and that's why I was often picked out to have these hushed conversations behind the scenes.

But I felt stuck.

What advice could I possibly give? I definitely wasn't going to ask them to stay and give up their newfound cognitive curiosity just because it would offend some in the more traditional corners of the church. So, truth be told, I was sneaking these intellectually hungry minds out the back door and telling them to follow the truth wherever it led them. I reasoned that if we equate God and Truth, an intellectually honest pursuit had to lead to God at the end of the day, and if the church was uncomfortable with things like facts, science, and verifiable truths, then perhaps God didn't live here anymore. Suffice to say, it wasn't a popular point of view, and there's no mystery as to why I didn't last in that particular profession.

So, in that assignment asking us about the "church and its relevance in the modern era," I railed about all this for a good 4,000 words, and I didn't pull any punches. I attacked the church for its antiquated ideas and its propensity to vilify the intellect and set it at opposition to faith. I was angry that I was losing so many good kids who no longer felt welcome in the institution I was supposed to represent, and their only crime was learning. I was mad about it all, and I let anyone who would be unfortunate enough to read that assignment know it in no uncertain terms.

I handed in the paper to Vic's office only to be called in after class the very next day.

I gingerly knocked on the door, having a fairly good idea of why I was in trouble. He opened it and wordlessly motioned for me to take a seat. We sat in opposite-facing leather wing-back chairs and just stared at each other for what felt like an eternity as he took his customary extended pause, with his forefinger pressed to his lips, while he worked out how he wanted to begin.

He eventually said, "Sean, I read your assignment. Between you and me, you're not wrong, but I'm not concerned with the content of what you said. I'm concerned about you."

I was a little taken aback, so I asked, "How so?"

He simply responded, "You're very angry, Sean."

"Of course I am," I said, and then I launched into an impassioned verbal recap of some of the finer points from the assignment. I even went so far as to say it baffled me that everyone else wasn't as angry as I was. How could everyone accept this ridiculous situation? Vic just calmly weathered this verbal hurricane with the patience of a saint and waited for me to burn myself out. I eventually spoke myself to a standstill, and he again made me wait before he simply said:

"Sean, I think you need to learn to *grieve humanity.*"

And then he dismissed me.

I was even more incensed after that. If he agreed with me, why was he acting as if the problem was my emotional response to a very obvious issue and not the issue itself? And "grieve humanity?" What the hell did that mean?

For the next couple of weeks, that phrase reverberated in my brain. Vic had planted something in me and I couldn't shake it. "Grieve humanity" came echoing back to me any time there was a moment of stillness, and as the days wore on, its meaning slowly started to take shape.

Why would I need to grieve humanity?

As I thought about it, I realised Vic was suggesting that there was something to mourn about us—all of us, collectively and individually, none of us exempt. We are all broken and wounded in some way. Things aren't as they should be. Chaos is always present.

As I thought about this, I realised that we all know this stuff deep down, and we're all fearful of being seen as defective or broken. So we play myriad games to protect ourselves, and many of those can be self-serving and cruel as we lash out or push others away and, in the process, end up hurting those around us and adding to their wounds.

That cycle deserves our grief.

Vic had clearly seen that my anger toward those in the church was grounded in my belief that there are "good" and "bad" people in the world. I was a "good" one fighting the good fight, and the leaders of the institution were the "bad" ones. He had also recognised that I took it personally when they wouldn't listen to me and when they attempted to sideline or sanction me for my ideas. But if I began to grieve humanity, it meant I needed to grieve for them too. I needed to understand that even though they were older than I was and in leadership positions, they were also scared and protecting their wounds. Their fear was driving them to ward off any change or progress because they were terrified of being exposed, and it had nothing to do with attacking me or those young minds in my care. That simple two-word phrase made me realise for the first time that people's hurtful actions are almost always about their fear and brokenness.

Most attacks are actually defence.

I began to replay my life in my mind and consider every offence I had taken; every school bully, every abusive family member, every relationship betrayal now looked different through this lens, and something softened in me. I realised that we are all just a mess, and we're trying to get by in the midst of our deep fears of each other. That doesn't mean that people don't do bad things that need addressing, nor that my points about the church needing to change weren't still valid, but I now didn't take it so personally. I was able to see the problems but also have compassion for everyone involved, which let me off my own emotional hook, while helping me approach the problem in a much more constructive way.

I wasn't exempt from all this, either. Those two words, "grieve humanity," also helped me see and acknowledge my own shadow for the first time. Getting honest with myself, I realised that by spending so much energy trying to appear perfect and not letting anyone see the chinks in my armour, I might be hurting others in this pointless pursuit. I had wounds I was protecting. I had impulses I was ashamed of. I had deep fears about how I was perceived by those around me.

I had a Shadow and it was time to face it.

&

Every photographer knows the importance of shadows.

Every image is made up of captured light and shadow. We are drawn to the light, but it's the shadows that sculpt the light into the shapes we recognise. Without shadow or the absence of light, we would just be looking at a blank piece of paper. Shadows give the light its boundaries and its form. Whether it's a smooth, gradual transition from light to shadow or a hard and sudden edge that separates highlights and shade, shadows hold the light in its frame and help us recognise what we're looking at.

In short, shadows are a photographer's best friend.

Like a photograph, we as artists are all a mixture of light and shadow—and we need to embrace our shadows in order to become better-rounded human beings with richer stories to tell. If we pretend to be perfect in the ways we project ourselves, we stand the real danger of creating work that comes across as "one-note." Rich work emanates from rich interiors, and nuanced art comes from those who own and access every part of who they are.

Carl Jung talked a lot about this aspect of our psyche, suggesting that we have both a Persona and a Shadow.

The Persona, he suggested, is the part of ourselves we want the world to see. It's those traits we are proud of that we push to the front and centre in all our interactions, hoping people will buy the implausible lie that these good qualities are the whole picture.

The Shadow, by contrast, is the part of ourselves that we are ashamed of or fearful of admitting exists in us. It contains our basest impulses and darkest thoughts, which we try to hide from the world for fear of what they will say.

Jung suggested that the road to becoming a well-rounded human being was to roll the Shadow into the whole—to own it, accept it, and add it to who we are as a person. He called this "integrating the Shadow." This is hard for most of us because we labour under the false assumption that to be accepted we need to hide our flaws. From childhood onward, we are taught to quash our darker impulses in order to fit in. Our families direct our actions early on, and then society sanctions us if we don't fall in with accepted norms, so we repress the sides of ourselves that we aren't sure about. However, trying desperately to impress and working to hide significant parts of our nature usually means that we are denying broad areas of our authentic self that need integrating.

As Jung said, "I'd rather be whole than good."

The need to have others see us as "good" can lead us to deny our natures, which will have an effect on the things we make. We may find ourselves creating things once again just to please the masses instead of honestly making the things that are unique to us. Just like with the example of Munch's painting *The Scream*, we have to look our Shadow in the face and own it completely before we can find the courage to share it with the world and potentially weather the storm of public opinion.

I know that my personal Shadow contains simmering low-level anger. I have to own that. It's a part of me and so should be a part of the things I make, but I still have the adult responsibility to point that anger in a positive direction. If I use it to bully those weaker than I or take out my frustrations on others as a way of self-medicating my resentments, then I've lost my way. However, if I own who I am, every part of me, and learn to turn that anger into fuel to talk about being human in all its messy complexity, I can make "good" use of a potentially "bad" quality.

After that conversation with Vic in his office that day, and the following month when I allowed those two words to do their work, the tone of my frustrations shifted. I don't think I was suddenly less angry, but I had seen my anger for what it was and I'd worked out where it was insecure and selfish. I still wanted to change things as much as ever, but now I had to call myself out on the worst of my motives around the anger I felt and feed the best of my intentions around the same.

The talks I gave in churches began to change in tone. Before this breakthrough, I wouldn't have had the courage to challenge the status quo because I hadn't faced my own anger. I often chose to bite my tongue onstage, knowing that I stood a good chance of my Shadow being revealed if I rocked the boat, but now that I had begun to admit I had a Shadow and even taken steps toward befriending it, I could disentangle myself from the emotion and more clearly see the good fight to be fought through my public speaking. I started talking from pulpits about our irrelevance to the modern world, our awful treatment of the poor in our communities, and our "high-horse homophobia" which was anything but loving. I talked about how we seemed to be building higher walls, figuratively and literally, to keep out the inconvenient truths about the world so that we could get on with the business of the insular clubhouse we had built for ourselves. Again, not a popular message, as you can imagine.

One day I was told by a church leader that my frustration with the institution wasn't "Christlike." Not long before, that challenge would have been enough to get me to run away and hide, but now things were different. I knew that anger was a part of me, and it was something I had accepted. So, instead of backing off, my response was that I believed I wasn't "Christlike" *enough*. I reminded him that passages like John 2:14-16 describe Jesus being so enraged that people had turned the temple of his day into a marketplace that he chased everyone out with a whip he had fashioned on the spot. Jesus got angry, and it's one of his traits that is rarely spoken about in sermons. We choose instead to think of him as the guy with the beatific smile who hugs lambs in paintings. In fact, throughout the Gospels, Jesus saves his choicest insults for the religious leaders of his day because they had similarly become inward-focussed and self-serving, having lost their love and concern for the real people around them. He pulled no punches in letting them know his opinion. So it seemed to me that, in actuality, I wasn't yet "Christlike" enough in my frustration, but I promised to work on it.

I managed to take my creative outlet at the time, public speaking, and carefully incorporate my particular Shadow. I started to choose against the destructive, selfish, insecure edge my anger sometimes had but still allowed that impulse to fuel the talks I wrote. I didn't yell. I wasn't rude, but I allowed people to see how I felt about the things I was discussing without shame that people would judge me for not being a perfectly stone-faced and stolid communicator.

It's important to say that we're not talking about self-indulgence here. It would be very easy to just look at our worst traits, refuse to change them, and expect everyone else to deal with them, but that's not "integrating your Shadow."

Anger is never an excuse for violence.

Lust is never an excuse for lechery.

Shame is never an excuse for self-harm.

Jealousy is never an excuse for spite.

No one is suggesting for a minute that we should unleash our basest impulses and wreak havoc on ourselves and those around us. I think our guiding principle should still be to "do no harm," and there is a huge difference between honestly looking our own darkness in the face and lovingly accepting ourselves anyway, and allowing those darker impulses to cause pain in the real world because we selfishly refuse to change.

The point is always to see your Shadow, turn it over, analyse it, take the good parts and tweak the bad. That way you can redeem the part of yourself that you previously felt you had to hide. Ironically, I think it's those who repress their Shadows who end up doing the most harm because, just as they don't own their Shadow self, they also don't take responsibility for the actions and destructive tendencies that originate there. However, facing and redeeming your Shadow will mean that you're aware of its motives and thus can redirect its energy and take full responsibility for your actions through a more complete self-awareness.

This is the process of becoming a better-rounded, more integrated human being and a properly integrated artist who has owned and accepted every part of themselves. This is the path to richer work. When we have rolled in those parts of ourselves that we have sought to repress, we will have more to say, and our message will become more nuanced and multifaceted, filled with more capital "T" Truth.

Leonard Cohen and Johnny Cash couldn't write many of the songs they did without having faced their Shadows.

Confessional poets like Robert Lowell, Anne Sexton, Sylvia Plath, and John Berryman could write the work they did only by looking their own darkness in the face.

I don't think Caravaggio could have spent hours working on *Judith Beheading Holofernes*, nor Rubens on *Massacre of the Innocents*, nor Goya on *Saturn Devouring His Son* without internally "grieving humanity."

Thank goodness these great artists all faced and embraced their Shadows and gave us work that more fully describes the experience of being human.

It's not just the Shadows within us but also the shadows we walk through that give us the content for our work. If we think about our life laid out before us, we will see patches of light and patches of shadow that make up our story, and just like every image needs a mix of both, an interesting story must have both light and shade.

We all, by default, would rather avoid the difficult times in our lives. When things are tough, I'm often tempted to zone out, put myself on autopilot, or dull my senses until things get better. If you gave me a fast-forward button that I could use to skip to a time when this current trial was over, I would be very tempted to use it, but I've learnt that skipping over the shadows would rob me of good growth.

Spiritual traditions around the world agree that the times in our lives when we are changing and growing in the most profound ways are most often in the shadows. When things are going well, we can coast, but when things get tough, we are forced to question, adapt, change, and expand. It's not the good times in our lives that shape us; it's the hardships we face.

We are forged in the shadows.

We adapt faster when there are problems to solve than when everything is going well. We learn more from good criticism than from good compliments. We develop faster through our failures than our successes. We find new strength when we are going through great pain. Just like working out in the gym, resistance defines and refines us.

So I'm slowly learning to be more present to the troubles of my life. Yes, they are and always will be painful. I can't avoid that, but mentally "checking out" of the situation will ensure that I miss the lessons that these particularly painful episodes have to give me. If I want to talk about the diversity of the human experience in my work then I also have to live the human experience fully, and that includes this current shadow I might be passing through.

We need to find the courage to be present to all of life in its full tonal range of light and shade. How else are we going to describe the Chaos to others if we don't allow ourselves to experience it? How will we point to the Order if we don't experience its absence in all its fullness?

Werner Herzog, who I've already mentioned in this book, is one of my favourite filmmakers. His films have a very bleak and unique tone, admittedly heightened by his melancholy voice-overs. While he was making *Fitzcarraldo* in the early 1980s in the jungles of Peru, he also had a documentary film crew capture behind-the-scenes footage. This material was later cut together and released as the film *Burden of Dreams*.

The topic of the documentary was the cost of having a dream, like wanting to make a film in which a steamboat is dragged over a mountain in the Amazon and not being able to let go of the idea that it needs to be done literally, with a full-size steamboat, and filmed with no special effects. The production of *Fitzcarraldo* was plagued with injuries, actor tantrums, cast and crew mutinies, extreme weather, and political unrest in the region, not to mention the obvious logistical nightmare of dragging a real steamboat over a very real mountain. But the part of the documentary that stood out for me was a short soliloquy Herzog delivers while standing alone in the jungle. On-screen there are shots of flowers, and frogs, and insects going about their lives, accompanied by the calls of exotic birds in the trees. It looks and sounds so picturesque and peaceful, so it comes as no small surprise when Herzog begins to talk and says:

Taking a close look at what's around us, there is some sort of a harmony. It is the harmony of overwhelming and collective murder, and we in comparison to the articulate vileness, and baseness, and obscenity of all this jungle; we only sound and look like badly pronounced and half-finished sentences out of a stupid suburban novel, and we have to become humble in front of this overwhelming misery, and overwhelming fornication, and overwhelming growth, and overwhelming lack of order. Even the stars appearing in the sky look like a mess. There is no harmony in the universe. We have to get acquainted with this idea that there is no harmony as we've conceived it. But when I say this, I say this full of admiration for the jungle. It is not that I hate it, I love it. I love it very much. But I love it against my better judgement.

I think you'll agree that this is a million miles from the mellifluous tones and upbeat outlook of Sir David Attenborough's voice-over work when he speaks about the same natural world. Herzog's work is probably not to everyone's taste, but I for one find his point of view so rich, so unexpected, so unusual, so iconoclastic that it forces me to take notice and presents a much more colourful and nuanced picture of life in its full spectrum.

I tell you this because, when you hear about Herzog's childhood and the shadows he had to pass through, his unflinching view of life's complexity makes a great deal more sense.

Born in the early years of the Second World War, he fled with his mother to the mountains after an Allied bomb hit the house next to their own in the city of Munich. From Herzog's account, she had to pull his tiny body from under-

255

neath a pile of glass and rubble. That was the last straw. She moved her family to the tiny Bavarian mountain village of Sachrang, where she hoped things would be safer until the conflict wound down. They had no running water, no flush toilet, and no telephone. As a child, Herzog had no toys to play with but didn't seem to wallow in what we would see as his misfortune, instead seeming to take joy in the blissful anarchy children in the community experienced in the absence of their fathers, who had all gone off to fight.

With the war winding down, he would live through one of Germany's most desolate eras with widespread poverty and economic hardship. He even recalls people being so desperate for food that they would peel the wallpaper from the walls to eat the glue behind it because it was rumoured to have some scant nutritional value. At the age of 12, he moved back to Munich, but the country was slow to recover. He wouldn't make his first phone call until he was 17 years old, but through sheer grit and determination, and working night shifts as a welder in a steel factory to get funds, he would begin making his first feature film only two years later.

This is a man acquainted with sorrow and hardship, and he's allowed those experiences to elevate his work. Telling him to just "think more positively" would be ridiculous and insulting. He has seen and lived life in all its joy and pain, and this nuanced worldview comes through in everything he makes, and as someone who gets tired of the often-forced positivism in much of filmmaking and media, I for one find his approach deeply captivating and searingly honest. It's those dark and painful seasons in his life that have undoubtedly coloured his outlook so that he now makes some of the richest and most challenging documentaries out there. Of course, there is a place for work that focuses solely on the joys of living, but we also need the balance or we run the risk of creating saccharine and anaemic art that doesn't capture the complexity and multiplicity of life as we all know it.

Some of the most compelling works of art are made by artists who are going through and describing a dark time in their lives.

How many songs have been written because of the heartbreak left after a relationship has ended? You can't do that well unless you are present to the pain you're experiencing. Songwriters who take us into their heartache are inviting us to walk through the shadows they have experienced, even if just for three minutes. When we hear those songs and can tell they've come from a genuinely broken heart, we can find comfort in our own heartbreak, knowing that this has happened to millions of others before us, and they made it through, so we can too.

The blues as a genre of music was birthed out of the pain of slavery, as a people cried out in their collective anguish and were present to their hardships. Field workers in the Deep South of the United States took their traditional African music and combined it with their daily work songs and their nightly spirituals to form a new category of music that has gone on to spawn other genres such as jazz and R&B and many elements of rock, pop, dance, funk, hip-hop, and soul. So much of our modern music owes a debt to the artists who managed to create out of the very real shadows they lived through.

Great artists learn to live their pain because they know it will enrich their work as they channel their experiences through paintbrushes and pen strokes, through piano keys and vocal cords, all the while being as present to their difficulties as a raw nerve. What would it mean to plumb the depths of the hardest stretches of your journey and, through your work, tell us what it taught you?

When we pass through those shadows, it's easy to become all-consumed by overwhelming emotion and shut down, but what if, in those moments, we threw our perspective a little wider to see the trajectory of our whole lives and remind ourselves of the big picture we are creating? Remember, it takes both light and shadow to make a good image, so this shadow we are wrestling with isn't the whole story, nor is it the end; it's only a tiny portion of the story we're telling. As difficult as it feels to bare now, we may look back and be grateful for the tone this current hardship added to our lives and the person it turned us into. That perspective likely won't make those difficult times any easier when they come, but hopefully, the perspective about the overall image you're creating with your life will help you to stay open, to learn from those difficult times, and to muster the courage to push through. We need shadows to live a good story, but as essential as those shadows are, their purpose is always to point us toward the light.

&

Scientists have done a number of studies to work out what human beings are drawn to in any given image.

By strapping on a pair of special goggles that track eye movements in a test subject, they can create heat maps to display which areas the average human eye spends the most time looking at when taking in a given photograph. As a photographer, I find this information incredibly useful because it helps me arrange the elements in a picture in a more deliberate way, composing them so that I can walk a viewer through an image as intended, using psychology to predict how someone will experience my work and even the path their eye movement is most likely to take.

Scientists discovered that people generally spend most of their time looking at either the most saturated colour, the area of highest contrast, any human faces present, and most dominantly, the brightest part of the image.

That last finding is especially interesting to me. It suggests that there is something hard-wired into the human brain that always looks for the light. I use this fact all the time in my work; as a portrait photographer, I've learnt that I need to pay special attention to my background. There is no point in taking a portrait in which the subject's face is dimly lit, but the background is filled with distracting highlights. The fact that we are involuntarily drawn to the human face because of ingrained pattern recognition may be trumped in this instance by the human habit to look toward the light. I'm not suggesting that portraits should always be shot with darker backgrounds, but that if you have a bright and busy background, you do run the risk of viewers looking longer behind and around the subject than you may like. Understanding the psychology helps me make stronger images.

In my standard portraits, I want the face to be bright and would only hide a subject's face in darkness with a bright background as a specific creative choice.

I especially want the eyes to be filled with light so that they draw you in. I work hard when lighting my subjects to make sure not only that light floods the lower iris to make the colour pop but also that there is a reflection in the upper half of the eye giving a life-infusing catchlight.

As much as we need the shadows to make good images (and I love a shadowy portrait more than most), we also need those points of light that draw the eye of our viewer. As I alluded to in the "Logos" chapter, Rembrandt created some of the most compelling portraits of all time, and even though he embraced shadows with the majority of his canvases being covered with dark and muted tones, he was also incredibly deliberate about making the face one of the brightest elements in any frame, often placing a cheeky dot of near-white paint in the corner of his subject's eyes. There are few artists who better exemplify this idea of shaping with shadows to accentuate the light.

&

If we all have Shadows that we need to face and integrate, we also have light within us that we need to celebrate and share.

One of my biggest gripes with the institutional church was the theological concept of "original sin," which has been peddled as truth by many since way back in the third century. This twisted notion suggests that we are all born evil, bad, corrupt, and marred and that human beings are in need of rescuing from minute one of their dirty existence. Not only is this idea not found in Scripture, but I think it was dreamed up as a manipulative mechanism to get people to fear their own darkness and cling to the church. It was really just an ancient formula that mirrored our modern era marketing strategy which suggests that, "You are flawed and lacking, but fear not, we have this thing that will make you whole."

How much damage has this corrupt concept done, in particular to Western psyches who have lived under this wayward belief for centuries? Perhaps you have never darkened the door of a church yourself, but I guarantee that shades of this idea have seeped into your thinking and self-image regardless because many versions of the same lie are so prevalent in our culture at large. We too often see ourselves as fundamentally wanton, depraved, and unworthy of redemption. I think it explains why we are so quick to devalue ourselves and why, in the modern era, our self-worth is at an all-time low.

We have to undo this idea and start with an appreciation of life and the cosmic fortune of our very existence. We need to get back to celebrating the miracle of both collective life and our individual lives. You were born good, pure light against the darkness, an act of Order appearing in defiance of Chaos. Recognising your own light is job one because you can't share it with others if you don't see it, and you won't be able to appreciate it in others if you can't see it in yourself first.

I almost skipped over all this in writing this book, but I don't want to take for granted that you know you are good. We so often focus on our faults and failures, and we allow our Shadows to overwhelm us. We attach so much emotional weight to the ways in which we don't measure up to some ideal that we forget to revel in the goodness of who we intrinsically are. We all have things we need to sort out within ourselves, but the fact still remains that life is a miracle, and you are that life. Your very existence and all life around you is the light that needs to be celebrated, and our goal in our work should always be to point to that light.

It's the near-rapture at the crescendo of a symphony performed by a skilled orchestra that lets us feel the grandeur of life without having to understand it.

It's the Turner landscape in its riot of almost formless colour that allows us to mentally bathe in the warmth of a sunset even on a crisp, cold day.

It's the soaring works of architecture, from the stone-columned forests of the great cathedrals to the winged phoenix now rising triumphant from the World Trade Center Transportation Hub, that give us a mixture of awe and hope.

It's the childlike marvel of an unsuspecting audience at the mercy of a street magician that lets them dream of Order beyond known-Order, and of all the mysteries we are yet to discover.

It's the flowing marble undulations of the ancient and medieval sculptors that stir us to quietly celebrate the beauty and sensuality of the human form.

It's the chef who works not only to provide technical culinary excellence but also to evoke feelings of a mother's love and care in making us a meal.

It's the twinkle in the eyes of Rembrandt's subjects amidst a sea of darkness that whisper of the resilience and brilliance of life.

❧

In our own journeys too, it's important to hold onto the light in order to preserve our motivation. As important as it is to be present to those shadow periods of our lives, staying too long and wallowing in darkness will always see us stalled. We also need to be present to those seasons of light to bring balance.

If you pay attention to the visuals you see when watching the work of great cinematographers, you will notice that they always work hard to preserve their highlights. Your average camera doesn't come close to being able to simultaneously resolve the same range of tones as the human eye, so filmmakers have to make a decision about which end of the limited dynamic range a camera can see to let go of. You could choose to blow the highlights and bring out some of the details in the shadows, but the vast majority of cinematographers say "no." Most choose to "embrace their shadows" and "protect their highlights." It's often a sign of an amateur filmmaker that they haven't yet learned how to preserve the details in their skies behind their subjects during daytime shots. This is especially true when shooting on modern digital cameras because when you blow your highlights beyond a certain point, the sensor no longer collects information in those areas. It just gives up and creates a field of empty white pixels where no amount of detail can be recovered, no matter what digital wizardry you apply in post-production. So modern photographers and filmmakers know how aware they need to be of blowing their highlights.

This idea of "embracing my shadows" and "protecting my highlights" has become a life philosophy for me. We covered the former, but let me just touch briefly on the latter.

Psychologists have known for a long time that the human mind has a negativity bias. That means that negative ideas, thoughts, and feelings mentally imprint on us much easier than positive ones do. The reason is a simple evolutionary one. When we lived on this planet as just another vulnerable animal without the advantages of our technologies to keep us safe, we had to be constantly hyper-aware of potential danger. Our brains developed so that every positive thought could be overridden, any daydream could be cut short instantly if we suddenly noticed a lion was stalking us through the long grass. The only focus at that point was to identify the danger and plan our escape. That meant that our brains evolved to be "crisis identifiers" and "problem-solving machines," and evolutionarily, it's served us well.

However, the good things in life don't usually require such immediate action and mental presence. As such, having a good harvest and feeling the impulse to celebrate could be immediately overridden when we realise the next tribe over is attacking and we have to defend ourselves, and even if that doesn't happen, we may still be worrying that it might in the near future, which would cut into our ability to celebrate in the now. Neurologically speaking, the negative can always cut into the positive, but the positive can't override the negative without great effort.

Psychologist Rick Hanson came up with the Velcro/Teflon concept to explain this better. He suggests that negative thoughts imprint on our minds like Velcro. It's an instant connection and one that is often hard to shift. However, the positive thoughts we have are like Teflon; they don't imprint in the same way as negative thoughts and often slide right off our consciousness. As a remedy, Hanson suggests that, now that we understand our brain's negativity bias, we need to be more conscious about giving positive thoughts the same chance to imprint as the negative thoughts, and that requires a conscious choice. He suggests that when we have that positive thought, we need to hold it deliberately in our minds for 20 seconds to allow it the same opportunity to neurally encode itself as the negative thoughts. This practice will bring us some balance.

For us and our journeys, that means celebrating today's successes as often as we can. As artists that means being quick to give ourselves the credit for the progress we are making or celebrate the particular project we just managed to complete. Our problem is that most of us are mental time travellers who insist on either feeding emotions like regret in order to dwell in our mental past, or feeding feelings like worry in order to live in our mental future. The problem is that, in the process, we miss out entirely on the light of each now. If we are choosing these past and future mental spaces instead of what is in front of us, then we can't be fed and refuelled by the good times we might be living through today.

The trick with all this is to find balance. We have to learn to live fully in the liminal—that confusing, complicated, and often uncomfortable space between past and future, and betwixt light and dark, where all life exists and the best pictures are made.

We have to "embrace our shadows," both the ones we pass through and the ones within us. We need to absorb everything they can teach us and use them to shape the light in our work and give it form.

I've done it with this book. I haven't shied away from talking about the shadows. I've spent time on "negative" subjects like Envy, our need for Attention, our habitual clutching for Control, and the worst impulses of our Ego, but I know that in being honest about our struggles, we will perhaps feel more encouraged to reach for the light together. I didn't want to write a book filled with positive platitudes and fridge-magnet-worthy sayings because, if you're like me, too much vacuous positivity doesn't help. I need my philosophy to be grounded in the light and dark reality of existence in order to believe it, and that means speaking about the shadows as much as the light, the Chaos as much as the Order.

But we must also "protect our highlights," both the ones within us and the ones we pass through. We need to remind ourselves of our intrinsic worth and enjoy the light of life in every now so that we can play that celebratory tone in our work and invite others to join in the refrain.

Meaning

On Christmas Eve about five years back, I was sitting at my desk in a big corporate office in London, staring out the window in a moment of reverie. I always opted to work over Christmas because, personally, I've never been too sentimental about the season, and I was happy to put in the hours so that other people could take some vacation days and visit loved ones. Besides, I loved the empty trains on my commute and the quiet offices when I arrived.

The offices in question belonged to a company that sold products online, and I had been hired to head up the photography department. After years of bouncing around as a freelancer, this full-time role and the financial stability that came with it were a welcome relief.

However, my photography was beginning to suffer.

When I began my photography career over a decade ago, I assumed I would have to pay my dues for a while with basic and repetitive photography work, but I had naively believed that when I reached a certain level (for example, "head of photography" for a big company), my inventiveness and imagination could be unleashed. After years of freelancing and struggling for work, I was looking for an oasis: a role that was creatively fulfilling but also comfortably paid the bills. I had hoped this latest role would be it, but it turned out to be just another mirage.

The truth was that I had no real control over the photography I was doing. The style of the company's imagery had been set long ago, and it had recently been made clear to me that there was no room for innovation. Ultimately, my job was to serve the company and the shareholders with my camera, but I was having to face the fact that my creativity was stagnating in this context as a result. That was all in the contract so I knew what I was potentially signing up for.

The fact that my photography was suffering was entirely my fault. I had forgotten the reasons I picked up a camera in the first place. It had just become a tool to make money during office hours, and I had forgotten the joys of self-expression. Getting honest with myself, I realised I had been so caught up in work that it had been an age since I had made time to experiment, play, and create for myself with a camera. As I sat there at my tinsel-bedecked desk in the middle of that deserted office floor, sipping my coffee, avoiding my emails, and staring out the window at the last-minute Christmas shoppers, a question formed in my mind.

What did I want photography to mean to me, beyond the day job? I knew that for me there wasn't enough meaning in making images of products to help people buy things from websites. I wanted more than that for my creative pursuits, and I knew that this was work I would have to do in my own time.

Human beings are "meaning-machines." We crave purpose in our lives.

In Viktor E. Frankl's landmark book, *Man's Search for Meaning*, he recounts his traumatic experiences being held in German concentration camps during the Second World War. He tells stories of those who survived the horrors of those camps and those who didn't. Beyond the obvious reasons for people's lives being cut short in those camps, he also observed that many of his campmates simply passed away because they lost hope. He also recounts for us the stories of those who didn't give up and insisted on persevering. As a therapist himself, he theorised that those who managed to find meaning for themselves, even in the presence of such horror and Chaos, were the ones who preserved their courage and the will to live on. He even boldly suggested that any pain or hardship in our human existence can be surmounted if we find purpose in the midst. In one passage he says, "Those who have a 'why' to live can bear with almost any 'how,'" and this came from a man who had endured some of the most atrocious "hows" any human in the past century has had to live through.

Whether we're in the midst of the light, or walking through the shadows, human beings need meaning. And if meaning isn't apparent in some areas of our lives, particularly in our work as makers, we will likely hit a point, as I did on that Christmas Eve, where we've built loads of creative skills in our chosen artistic outlet and are left asking ourselves what the meaning in all this is. What are we supposed to use this newly developed creative voice for? What is the point of being an accomplished pianist, or painter, or poet? Is it just to get famous or make money, or is there more to it than that?

There is, of course, nothing wrong with aiming for fame or fortune in themselves, but for most of us, that doesn't constitute "meaning." Finding the meaning in the making is something more, and if we discover it for ourselves, it will gift each one of us with an endless well of vitality, motivation, and direction, no matter who we are or where we find ourselves in our journey.

So how do we find the meaning in our making?

For years, stretching back to my time working for the church, I've been guided by this quote from Frederick Buechner, and even though I am less ecclesiastically inclined these days, I think it holds deep capital "T" Truth for those of us searching for meaning:

"The place God calls you to is the place where your deep gladness and the world's deep hunger meet."

&

Let's start with your "deep gladness."

I don't want to assume that you know what that is for yourself, but I imagine if you've picked up this book that you are already someone who has a specific creative pursuit or maybe multiple art forms you practice that bring you joy.

However, maybe you aren't sure yet because you're still exploring. You know that making things brings you joy in general, and perhaps you've been dipping your toe into a series of artistic media, but you haven't yet settled on one to focus on.

Or perhaps you have already found one specific creative outlet, but you're struggling to find your focus within that medium. Maybe you've fallen in love with photography, for example, and you've tried a bit of everything, but you're not sure whether to focus on developing your landscape photography or your street photography.

If your "deep gladness" is half of the equation to finding meaning in your work, then it's worth taking the time to find out what it is that brings you the most joy and fulfilment. Professor Joseph Campbell called this "following your bliss."

Campbell's particular "bliss" was the study of myths, religions, and stories told by human beings around the globe. He made it the work of a lifetime to catalogue those myths and share them in his voluminous work *The Masks of God,* and he then went on to examine the commonalities of the stories we tell in his book *The Hero with a Thousand Faces.* He believed that by studying the stories we tell, we can see patterns emerge and even come up with a "monomyth" or template for all myths. That structure would then tell us a great deal about what we have collectively intuited about the human journey beyond the specific era or cultural location of our birth.

He was especially interested in the stories we tell about heroes because he posited that our "hero stories" contain our ideas about what makes a meaningful human life. Campbell's model of "the hero's journey" has been used more deliberately in storytelling ever since he first shared it with the world, especially amongst Hollywood scriptwriters, because there is something in this innate structure that resonates with us. The very basic version goes something like this:

An inciting incident occurs, and the status quo is thrown out of equilibrium. Chaos enters.

The hero is then forced to leave the relative safety of home in order to attempt to restore balance.

The hero goes on a journey in which they encounter mentors who give them advice and companions who will assist the hero by applying their gifts to the tasks ahead.

The hero then goes through a series of trials and temptations until they face the final challenge.

In battling the final adversary, they also realise they must battle an element of themselves to overcome the Chaos and reset some Order.

As the dust settles, they find that the final test has left them irrevocably changed.

At the close of most hero stories, we see them return home to bring back a gift or "boon" to the community. The gift may be something totemic, or it may be the gift of themselves now that they have been refined by the shadows of their journey.

Campbell was obsessed with this metanarrative, this "monomyth." These are the common elements of the stories we tell, and he was especially interested in what it could show us about ourselves. He believed that in understanding the stories we share with one another, we could better understand how to create purpose and meaning in our own journeys, and he suggested that the key to getting started was to "follow your bliss" because that will give you your compass bearing.

In 1988, about six months after Campbell's death, PBS aired a prerecorded, six-part interview with him and Bill Moyers. In part four Campbell speaks about "bliss," saying:

If you follow your bliss, you put yourself on a kind of track that has been there all the while, waiting for you, and the life that you ought to be living is the one you are living . . . Follow your bliss and don't be afraid, and doors will open where you didn't know they were going to be.

I know that will sound a little sentimental to some, but I believe it's true. If we accept that we are each uniquely constructed, then our individual joys are hard-wired in us just like our individual personalities and peccadillos, and finding those joys is surely the route to finding our purpose. Your "bliss" is that deep sense of where your soul wants to go.

This is where we have to come back to allowing ourselves to intuitively follow our gut and "feel" our way forward because it's rarely the case that we can consciously work out the direction of our bliss from the minute we start looking for meaning. To find the right path, we have to intuit where our joy lies and follow it—and not let anyone put us off once we've found it. It's always the beginning of finding meaning.

Your bliss is not just self-indulgence, though. Finding your bliss will usually mean there is now a great deal of work in front of you, or a long "hero's journey" ahead to bring meaning to your making. Campbell was reportedly a little dismayed in his later years of lecturing, when some of his students decided that he was advocating hedonism as a lifestyle, but word has it that in response to this misinterpretation, Campbell remarked, "I should have said, 'Follow your blisters.'" Your bliss is the beginning of the path, not an end in itself, and the path ahead will require a great deal of exertion and effort to arrive at meaning as a destination, but identifying your "deep gladness" will show you where to place your first steps.

It is also your best chance at producing work that is new and fresh. You are unique in your interests and singular in your mental composition. You are a one-of-a-kind mix of character, worldview, temperament, aptitude, and disposition, and if you can find it within yourself to tap into your deep gladness in such a way that it incorporates every part of who you are, then the things you make will be unique to you. We're not just talking here about picking an art form to engage in; we're talking about working out all the things that bring you deep joy and effectively rolling them into the things you make.

Let me use myself as an example. Obviously, I have chosen writing, photography, and filmmaking as the media that bring me deep gladness, but what should I be writing about, taking photos of, or making films about? Well, the next step for me is to work out where else my deep gladness abides and how I can turn the skills I've developed toward those passions. In my case, I am also fascinated by psychology, history, spirituality, and philosophy. These other joys of mine have influenced my writing, photography, and filmmaking and brought more meaning to my making.

I attempt to communicate what I know and feel about human beings through my portrait photography. I think deeply about the light and shadow in my images and apply the messages I've given in the previous chapters to my photographs when I speak about them. I want to dig deeper into longer-term projects that explore the psychology, spirituality, and philosophy of people from different cultures too, and this has all become a direction for me because I have attempted to combine my joys—both my love of photography and my love of philosophy.

My YouTube channel is a great example. There are countless photography channels online focussing on gear, and techniques, and general photography practices, but I wanted to start a channel that better represented the things I cared about. Photography is still the ostensible subject of my channel, but those who have watched will know that I am far more interested in talking about the philosophy behind our creativity, the "why" behind our choices of subject matter, and the psychology of staying motivated and in-spired. Paying attention to my deep joys, all of them, and choosing to incorporate as many as I could into the films I make, rescued me from producing another YouTube channel about cameras. There's nothing wrong with choosing to run a gear-focussed YouTube channel, of course, but in my case, going that direction would have amounted to missing an opportunity to build my own personality and the things I care about into my work. I'm not suggesting I've come up with something brand-new, but I am suggesting that the films I produce for that channel have a flavour all my own because I paid attention to all the things that bring me joy, and as such, they are filled with more meaning for me personally.

Even this book you're holding, which is far from a traditional book on creativity, is a result of my attempts to pay attention to all the things that bring me joy. I was advised by some to give more practical exercises or advice on these pages, but that wasn't the book I wanted to write. I didn't want to produce a how-to book; I wanted to write the book I would have wanted to read. I wanted to encourage and inspire you, all the while treating you like adults and trusting that you will know best how to apply this advice to your journey. Some will love a book like this, some may not, but this is my "bliss," and I have had to find the courage to write this book according to my own internal compass and then release it into the world.

Regardless of the feedback I get on my photography, my filmmaking, my writing, or anything else, I can honestly say that I can feel the meaning in this work more and more each day because I'm learning to trust my gut. Campbell spoke of "unseen hands" helping him along as he followed his bliss, and I think I know what he means. The more I learn to follow this internal leading, the more things seem to fit neatly into place.

So the first half of finding the meaning in your making is to identify your "deep gladness." Listen for those little hints of where your joy lies, but remember that your "joy" shouldn't be taken too literally. It may not manifest itself as simple happiness; it could equally appear as a compulsion to explore the shadow side of life, but your "joy" is always that road you feel compelled to take.

Ask yourself: When was the last time you were making something, and you completely lost track of time? Right there and then, when your unconscious mind takes over, that will be your creative voice in full flow, and it's worth coming back to what you were doing in those moments to explore it more.

Also ask: When was the last time you made something, and it just left you buzzing? When we are trying to force something that isn't true to us, it robs us of our energy, but conversely, when we are making things out of our "deep gladness," we will find that it gives energy back to us.

These are the green lights beckoning us on.

If you already know the answer and you are clear about what creative pursuit brings you that deep joy, the next step is to look wider and work out what else in your life draws you in. What are your interests? What subjects do you care about? What topics of conversation get you animated when they emerge in social settings? What do you like to read? What films do you like to watch? What music do you listen to? Are there themes that emerge there? The trick is now to take more of who you are, more of those topics that bring you joy, and to turn your typewriter, or your pen, or your paintbrush, or your pencil—or whatever your instrument—to those subjects and see if more meaning doesn't flow into your work.

Let's assume you've found that art form and you've begun to build your skill set. You've identified the other aspects of your personality that bring you deep gladness, and you're working out how to roll your broader interests into your creative output. Now, what do you point that work at, and what is your message? If your deep gladness is one half of the equation to finding the meaning in your making, then "the world's deep hunger" is the other.

Have you considered that the things you make might have the ability to change things around you?

Let me give you a few quick examples of photographers who seem to have found the intersection of their joy and the world's hunger.

Martin Usborne heard about the plight of the "galgo," or Spanish greyhound. For centuries this breed has been put to work as hunting dogs in rural Spain. They used to be prized by the nobility and protected by law, but in modern times it has been estimated that up to 100,000 aging galgos deemed no longer strong or fast enough to hunt are abandoned or killed at the end of each season. Many dogs are simply abandoned by the side of the road, but in acts of unthinkable cruelty, some are "punished" for their physical failures by being hung from trees or thrown down wells alive.

So Usborne decided to use his love of photography to make a difference. He travelled to Andalusia and partnered with two rescue centres to produce a series of images of abandoned galgos to share their tragic story with the world and hopefully make a difference in their plight by creating awareness—and even helping by raising funds. In addition, the classic approach in Usborne's images helps bring back some lost dignity to these beautiful animals. For me, his images masterfully ride the line between showing both the elegance of these animals and the desperation of their plight. His website says of the project:

This series does not look directly at the pain. The photographs show rescued dogs alongside the landscapes in which they are abandoned in a way that is inspired by the painter Velázquez who worked in the same area in which these images were taken and at a time when these dogs were still considered noble.

In his project *Where Hunting Dogs Rest*, Usborne has taken his deep gladness around photography, his love of artists like Velázquez, and his affection for animals and turned his camera toward this issue, taking something broken and Chaotic and, through his images, restoring some Order.

Tish Murtha lived in Newcastle upon Tyne in the late '70s and '80s during the mass closure of the coal mines and the disbanding of manufacturing jobs by the Thatcher government. She saw the area she called home go through incredible economic hardship, with services collapsing and unemployment soaring. She also noticed how many children were left to run through the rubble of the streets unsupervised during the day and wondered to herself what their future would look like with so few prospects and opportunities.

She had found her bliss in photography, though, and she began to train her camera on the problems she saw in her community. She had a particular affinity for the plight of children who grew up under difficult circumstances. She spent hours hanging out with them on the streets and in their homes, building relationships and gaining their trust. They weren't just subjects; they became collaborators in telling the story of their collective hardships. The images she took celebrated these tenacious, resourceful, clever, and resilient children, and apparently, Tish was always fiercely protective of them. This wasn't merely a job she had given herself to do. She genuinely cared.

She also felt an obligation to the people and problems within her local environment, and she believed that she could use her love of photography to highlight the real struggles of the people in her town. She used her camera like a megaphone to tell the world, "We're here, and this is what we're going through!" In fact, when Tish's pictures first appeared as an exhibition called *Youth Unemployment*, her local MP used those images in Parliament as evidence of the disturbing reality of life in the north of England, where so many were leaving school with little hope of work. Many were appalled at what they saw, and the images stirred a fierce debate in government. It's hard to measure how much those images were a catalyst for change, but one thing is certain, they got people talking.

Sebastião Salgado is one of my heroes in photography. He has spent a lifetime relentlessly filling his frames with the "world's deep hunger." His *Workers* project saw him travelling the globe to photograph steelworkers in the former Soviet Union, shipwreckers in Bangladesh, firefighters in the oil fields of Kuwait after the Persian Gulf War, fishermen in

Sicily, tea pickers in Rwanda, and most famously, gold miners in Brazil working in huge open pits.

His *Exodus* project took him to India, Vietnam, the Philippines, Ecuador, Palestine, Iraq, Yugoslavia, the Congo, and Rwanda to tell the heartbreaking stories of displaced peoples who had been forced to flee their homes.

Most recently, he has chosen to point his lens at the natural world. From 2004 to 2013, he produced a huge collection of images designed to show the natural beauty of our planet and celebrate a time before the ravages of man's industrialisation and mechanisation. He called the project *Genesis*. These images have been described as a "love letter to the planet" and serve as a reminder to humankind of our responsibility to maintain this beautiful world we call home and not to abuse our position as a species.

Alongside this mammoth photography project, Salgado and his wife, Lélia, took some of the money they had made from exhibitions and print sales and turned their hands toward restoring a patch of the natural world in their homeland of Brazil. Sebastião's grandfather had a farm there, but it had become a wasteland as the ground was slowly exhausted of its life-giving minerals. Sebastião and Lélia decided to take the 600 hectares and begin rebuilding the landscape by planting hundreds of indigenous plants in an effort to fill this little valley once more, restoring the forests that originally existed there. They succeeded so thoroughly that wildlife—including many species of bird, anteater, turtle, and even jaguar—have returned in recent years. The land has now been renamed the Instituto Terra and turned into a national park so that it belongs to all the people of Brazil, not to mention also serving as a model for reforestation worldwide.

The creative efforts of artists like Usborne, Murtha, Salgado, and thousands of others, have incrementally pulled Order from Chaos as they found the intersection of their "deep gladness" and the "world's deep hunger." I doubt many of them struggle with the question of meaning in their work. They might be frustrated that they can't do more and can't bring about the change they want to see faster, but I imagine that having discovered that sweet spot, each of them is keenly aware of their work's purpose and meaning.

I'm not suggesting that you need to become some sort of activist with your art, although you might want to, of course. There is nothing wrong initially with just setting the goal of paying your bills with the work you make, but once you attain that, and maybe even long before you do, you might seek more meaning in your work. And meaning may be found by pointing your work at something you consider worthwhile. This doesn't mean you need to "preach" with your work, nor is it equally possible to do so with every art form, but perhaps you can find a way to donate your time and artistic talent to people who are deserving, or start donating some of the proceeds to worthy causes. Whatever you choose, I guarantee that if you take this art form that brings you such personal joy and find ways to use it in support of others, it will be the missing piece that brings meaning to your work.

Many of us find the meaning in the message of our work. So much of art is communication, and we have to decide what we want to speak about. I wish I could just tell each of you what your message is, but finding out what you have to say is a deeply personal journey. No one can choose what your creative voice should sound like but you. No one can tell you what to care about because that has to come from your own worldview and concerns. So learn to pay attention to those subjects that perk you up when they arise in conversations. Ask yourself what you see in the world that you believe needs to change. Take a look at your life to see if you have access to stories that you believe need to be told. The message for your work could be lying in the answers to these questions.

If we think of Chaos as the breakdown of the things around us, then the way to create Order is to reconnect those broken things. Our work has the ability to mend those connections that have broken. In an interview with *National Geographic*, Usborne said of his portraits of the galgos:

I'm deeply concerned with the rift between humans and (other) animals and want to bring awareness to this painful divide. We are separated from other animals by language, technology, and a fatal arrogance that causes immense pain.

That's Chaos and "broken connection" language. Murtha's work reconnected a community with its dignity, and a parliament with its responsibility to its citizens. Salgado's work reconnected workers with their rights, and refugees with a place to call home as people took notice of their plight. His *Genesis* project has reconnected indigenous fauna and flora to the valley at the Instituto Terra in Brazil, and hopefully, his images contribute to our collective reconnection to this planet we call home.

By the way, all this "reconnection" used to be the job of religion. I know that for many "religion" is a dirty word, but let me reclaim it by showing you where it came from. Many have suggested that the word "religion" is derived from the Latin "ligare," meaning "to connect or bind." It's where we get the English word "ligament." When combined with "re," it brings us back again to this idea of "re-connecting." Good religion's job was meant to be remaking broken connections. Those involved were meant to reintroduce us to the divine. They were meant to reconnect us with ourselves and our own humanity. They were meant to build back the broken connections between families, friends, and nations, and their job was to reconnect us with this planet we live on and remind us of our responsibility to care for it.

I'll be the first to acknowledge that much of religion today does a poor job of this. Many institutional religions have become so wound up in the business of their insular groups that they've forgotten their bigger role. So I wonder if it's time for artists to step up and remake those connections for us, to help us reconnect with our own humanity, with one another, and with the natural world. If Chaos is the breakdown of connections over time, then Order is reestablishing those connections against the flow of entropy. In that sense, I hope for more "religious" artists who find their purpose and commit themselves to this "re-ligare" work of mending broken things. I believe our autonomic drive to find the meaning in our work is always pushing us in that direction. Those questions that inevitably surface in us and won't be silent are asking us to use our gifts for more than ourselves.

It's certainly been true for me. As I've said, these days my "deep gladness" is writing, speaking, photography, and filmmaking, but I also see a "deep hunger" in the world that has come to my attention because of my love for other things like psychology, spirituality, and philosophy. I'm then left wondering if, in bringing all these things together, I can remake some broken connections with my creative efforts.

Personally, it weighs heavily on me how many people are wrapped up and trapped in their own anxieties. Too many people these days are lost in despair and unable to see a way forward, and I know that a good life philosophy and a belief in one's own agency could do miracles for someone who feels lost and alone.

That's why I'm writing this book, and those are the concerns that have drawn me to talk about the topics I have.

That's why I'm drawn to portrait photography as a first love—I know it has the power to change the way you see yourself.

That's why my YouTube channel has the focus on philosophy and inspiration that it does. Every time I receive a message or an email from someone telling me how they have found their way again because of something I've shared, I feel the meaning in my making and once again remember my purpose. The idea that something I've made could make a difference to even one other person never fails to warm me.

This mindset helps me see art as service. If my creative abilities can help lift others out of their daily struggles and offer comfort, excitement, inspiration, direction, or joy, then I want those talents to be used for that purpose and not just for my own aggrandisement.

If you can find it within yourself to identify your "deep gladness" and point it at the "world's deep hunger" to remake the broken connections you see and pull Order from Chaos in the small ways you can manage, I have no doubt that you will find profound meaning in your making.

Time

Two years ago, I was sitting alone in a cabin in Iceland, staring out the window at the driving rain. I was willing the weather to improve so I could head out to take some photos and shoot the video I had planned for the trip, but the forecast said this storm would last for at least three of the five days of my getaway. So there was nothing I could do but hunker down, read a book, and drink too much coffee.

It also happened to be my 40th birthday.

Something about the marking of another year makes me a little wistful, and I usually end up taking some time in the day to look my life over, to celebrate and mourn the events that deserve either, and to ask myself whether I feel I'm moving in the right direction. It's also on birthdays that I allow myself a measure of nostalgia. These are the days that I end up looking up past friends and flames online to find out where they are and how they're doing, and it's on these days when I pull up old photos to reminisce about times gone by.

As the clouds thickened, the light dropped, and the sleet turned to flurries of snow, I started to think back to other birthdays. I tried to remember where I was and what I wanted out of life at each point.

I remember my 10th birthday back in Lesotho, where my mom had gotten me an ice cream cake in the shape of an aeroplane. She had recently taken up flying, and I wanted nothing more than to be a pilot like her one day. It would be a few years later in high school that I would discover I was deuteranomaly colour-blind, which would disqualify me from this particular dream. Apparently, it's fairly important to be able to tell the difference between flashing green and red lights in a pinch when flying an aircraft.

My 15th birthday was spent in Swaziland. At that time of my life, I had decided that I wanted to rehabilitate big cats and reintroduce them into the wild. After reading copious books by George and Joy Adamson, John Varty, Gareth Patterson, and Mark and Delia Owens, I knew I wanted to fight against the poaching trade and work with orphaned lions and leopards to see them returned to the bushveld where they belong. It wasn't until my first year at university, when I flunked my maths and chemistry exams and could no longer continue with a wildlife sciences degree, that this dream too had to be put to bed. So I switched to studying psychology and began to work for the church.

On my 21st birthday, I was in the Drakensberg mountains in South Africa and had decided that I wanted to be a pastor. I had finished my psychology degree and had just been accepted to seminary in Johannesburg, where I was due to start in a few months. It would be four years of study, then nearly a decade working for seven churches, before I realised that I was never going to fit into that institution and I needed to make yet another major course correction.

On my 30th birthday, I was living in Cape Town and had just been fired from the last church I would work for, for being a "liberal heretic." Truth be told, I'd received quite a few job offers from less conservative churches, but I had made the decision to stop banging my head against this particular brick wall. Enough was enough, and I had to admit that this wasn't a good fit. I had already been doing some video and photography work on the side, so it seemed worth taking the risk and finding out if I could make this my next career path. Friends of mine had booked my favourite coffee shop, and I remember everyone else chatting away as I sat slightly distracted, confident that I had made the right decision but equally worried about being able to make this new direction work.

My 37th birthday was spent in London, and at this point, I had worked full-time for a number of companies as an in-house photographer. The early years after the church had been a real struggle, and my main source of income for much of this time came from waiting tables at a local restaurant while I built up my photography skills and cut my teeth on low-paying freelance jobs. It had taken longer to get here than I had anticipated, but I was proud to have arrived at a position where I was paying all my bills with a camera in hand. But I wanted more and had recently decided to explore being a filmmaker. I began to plan how I would approach making videos, creating little documentaries, giving talks on-camera about subjects that mattered to me, and starting to sketch out what a YouTube channel could look like.

At 40, sitting alone in a cabin in the middle of Iceland, watching the light die and the storm intensify outside, I had established a three-year-old YouTube channel with a growing audience, yet as fulfilling as that work was, I also felt limited in terms of what I could talk about and the depth with which I could explore topics in shorter films. So, as I sipped my umpteenth cup of coffee and stared out the window at the petulant weather, I picked up my notebook and began to sketch out the first rough outline for the book you're holding.

Things change.

We put so much pressure on ourselves to get it right the first time. I remember feeling like a failure so often on my journey because so many of my dreams never materialised. As my goals changed from "pilot" to "wildlife conservationist" to "pastor" to "photographer" to "filmmaker" to "author," I had to get realistic and admit that life is full of twists and turns and rarely moves in the straight line we may wish it did. I've learnt since that in order to make ground, we don't have to bring every single dream to fruition, but instead, we have to be flexible and supple enough to pick ourselves up when we inevitably fail so that we can readjust and give ourselves new dreams to pursue.

The trick is to keep moving.

Our creative journeys are the same. You've heard me mention in this book that I've tried drawing, set design, music, public speaking, photography, filmmaking, and writing as creative media. Some of these skills have worked out and I keep them in my toolbox, but some haven't and have been left by the wayside. However, none of it has been a waste because no one medium needs to hold all the answers. My creative journey has unfolded in layers, and I believe it will continue to do so if I just keep moving.

The other thing I've learnt is that everything meaningful takes longer than we think it will, or should. Discovering your bliss, finding your creative voice, working out what you want to say, and carving out a context where you can do your work all takes time. If your path is anything like mine, it will be full of stops and starts, a mix of dead-end alleyways and long stretches of open freeway. But looking back, I can't see any other way it could have unfolded. Living through it was often incredibly frustrating, but now I've realised that this is how it works for most of us, which helps me accept the mystery of what comes next with more grace. Experience has taught me that if I'm patient enough and I keep moving, the next steps will emerge.

In order to shift our focus from anxiety over short-term successes to a longer-term vision for a meaningful creative life, we have to accept that it will take time. We stand more of a chance of making it to the destination and not giving up along the way if we learn to pack for the long road ahead. So let's have a look at how these things often evolve.

&

Carl Jung popularised the idea of the "two halves of life" as a way to describe the progression of human lives, using the analogy of a day split in half by the noonday sun. In the morning, the sun rises until it reaches its zenith at noon, and in the afternoon, it sets, neatly splitting our days in two. He suggested that understanding this progression is important because it can teach us how to respond to the various stages of our lives and to welcome the changes that will inevitably come as "good omens" instead of fearing them. Even though he spoke of these "two halves" in the context of our broader development as human beings, this idea can be applied as powerfully to our creative journeys.

Let's begin with Jung's "morning."

In the first half of life, he suggests, we are more focussed on building our sense of self and realising personal success. In this stage, we are concerned with things like getting ahead socially and building a successful profession. Thinking back to the chapter on "Ego," this is the time of life when we are working out who we are in the world and attempting to define ourselves so that we stand out in some way from the sea of humanity. There's nothing wrong with that; in fact, it's an important stage in our development that we shouldn't rush or attempt to skip.

The morning is also the time when we make lots of decisions about the sort of life we want to lead. We decide things like what job we want to do, who we would like to partner with, what sort of place we'd like to live in, what our politics are, what our life philosophy is, and what we believe about the world and the way it works. In his book *Falling Upward*, author Richard Rohr discusses the "two halves" dynamic in the context of our spiritual journeys and suggests that, in the morning, we construct "metaphorical boxes" that hold our ideas about the way we think life works in general, as well as the decisions we've made about how we want our own lives to play out specifically. This "box of answers" then acts as both our constructed worldview and our personal identity. This is all the work of the morning, and it's all good.

So what about our creative journeys?

Well, I think the morning of our journey with any art form is characterised by making decisions about the sort of artist we want to be and deciding what our work will look like, or sound like, or taste like. It's in the morning that we begin determining our style, and we do that by teaching ourselves loads of techniques, getting deep in the analysis of the gear we choose to use, and looking at the work of others to try and assess which elements we'd like to roll into our own mix. We are trying to delineate who we are as "makers of things" and work out what sets us apart. The mornings of our creative journeys are all about defining ourselves.

This phase is often very exciting. We are learning at a rapid pace and dreaming of what could become of our newfound creative pursuit. We are working out how to express ourselves in new ways, and it's always thrilling to get those early positive responses to our work from others. It was in the morning of my photography journey that I was driven to pick up my camera in any spare time I had. Every little photography mission I took seemed to teach me something new, and I fell deeper in love with this art form daily. That proved more than enough motivation to get me off the couch and working to improve my skills.

However, mornings can also be characterised by a great deal of frustration. I always wanted to be farther along than I was, and I was constantly looking for shortcuts to get there. My photography "morning" saw me spending hours and hours watching gear reviews, hoping that I could find a "magic lens" that would cover up the mistakes in my images and jump me forward to being a photographer with a recognisable style. I was constantly doing math with my meagre income, trying to work out how I could afford the fanciest cameras because I thought it would be a quick win in my development. Unfortunately, I talked myself into making a few of those lavish purchases and realised the obvious truth too late: bad images still look bad when taken with amazing cameras.

I spent loads of time watching video tutorials online and tried out every technique in the book, hoping that one would provide me with some easily won flair in my work and even gift me a fully formed "style" on a silver platter. From complicated lighting setups with coloured gels, to tilt-shift lenses and various filters, to Brenizer stitches, to endless preset bundles and heavy-handed editing techniques, I tried everything to define a look for my images that would make them stand out.

Of course, when I look back now, I can see what a visual mess I was making. But I also realise it was an entirely necessary mess. I don't know another way to learn but to try a bit of everything and start choosing for and against all those techniques until a more mature style emerges, and that takes time. I don't regret my early days of erratic experimentation because I learnt a great deal that I've brought along with me.

I only wish I could go back and tell myself to enjoy this phase more and not load it with such heavy expectation of quick success. I was constantly agitated that my creative voice wasn't emerging fast enough, and that's what led me to latch onto the lazy belief that fancy gear or convoluted techniques could be a shortcut. I now look back and realise that the work of building a genuine creative voice has to be the work of a lifetime and can never be purchased over a camera store counter, nor will it ever be discovered in a "top tips" video.

These experiments and this drive for definition is the good work of the morning. That's what it's there for, and looking back now I can see how essential this phase was in my growth as a photographer, and what a shame it is that I tried so hard to rush through it.

&

So how do we know when the morning of our journey is coming to its natural end? How do we know when we've hit "noon?" Jung was actually the first to talk about the idea of a midlife crisis in the way we understand it today, using this metaphor of "high noon."

In life, our noon is that point where we allow ourselves to stop long enough to take stock and ask ourselves whether everything we've been building all this time has been worth it.

Is it all pointed in the right direction?

Are we constructing the character we intend?

Are we becoming the human being we really want to be?

It's usually a time of difficult questioning, which, if we have the humility, often leads us to admit that we got some things wrong in the morning and we don't entirely believe in the person we've built for ourselves. Perhaps we've been so caught up in trying to hack the system and get ahead that we've spent our energies constructing the most expedient version of ourselves, instead of the most honest. Although this period can be quite difficult, we can't move into life's "afternoon" without directly facing these questions.

The noon of our journeys is often triggered by a crisis of some sort. Perhaps we lose our job, or our partner leaves us, or someone we love dies. Whatever it is specifically for each of us, it's often that painful event that provokes a lot of questions. We've been working so hard to define ourselves and build a life around that person who just left us, or that job we just lost, or that political worldview that has just been shattered, or that spiritual belief that doesn't seem so omniscient anymore. Now it's gone, and the world once again seems like an uncertain place, as Chaos overtakes our attempts at building Order into our lives.

So we turn to our box of neatly packaged beliefs about life that we put together in the morning, but those old, narrow ideas just don't hold any meaningful answers for us anymore.

We know too much now.

This is obviously a very scary moment for many, and some of us don't handle it well. You probably know the stereotype of a man in a midlife crisis, buying a motorbike and leaving his wife for a younger woman. Instead of admitting that deep down, the confusion he feels is pointing to the holes in the person he's built over time, he tries to rearrange the surface details of his life in the hopes that it will fix the problem. But, of course, it doesn't. You can't outrun those questions, and ignoring them simply guarantees that you will never move through to the afternoon of life.

Many choose denial and enter a sort of all-encompassing refutation of the questions that have surfaced, and if this position is held for too long, it can turn to bitterness in later years. Some shun change so drastically that they simply retreat into the box they built, reinforce it, and lock themselves in for good. An unwillingness to let what doesn't work fall apart and a lack of courage to begin building anew will keep us stuck in the morning. However, if we can begin to sort out the "good" from the "convenient" within the things we've built, then we can take noon as our cue to move into life's afternoon.

So what does the noon of our creative journey look like?

Well, in a similar fashion, the crisis point can come when we realise that all the energy we've put into learning techniques, obsessing over gear, and defining a style hasn't yielded the results we want. Perhaps we've struggled for years, yet our work still isn't as "popular" or as "successful" or as "meaningful" as we hoped it would be, whatever that means to us personally. We suddenly realise that the journey is more difficult than we thought, and the road is longer than we expected.

Our creative noon crisis might be something specific. I've had photographer friends whose crisis point arrived when all their camera gear was stolen, or they lost their job, or they had an illness or an accident and couldn't shoot the way they used to. They had to adjust and reassess what was really important in their work in order to move forward.

You know by now that in my own creative journey with photography, my noon crisis point appeared around the time I was staring out the window on that Christmas Eve in the previous chapter. I had put in all this work to teach myself fancy photography tricks and techniques, and I'd ploughed a load of money into purchasing gear, but it didn't satisfy me, and my work still felt empty.

I had to get honest with myself about a lot of uncomfortable things. I decided, for example, that I didn't really like the style I had built for myself. It was too complicated and fussy, and it was born of a desire to impress, rather than through developing a style that felt authentic to me. I was a photographer with lots of skills and nice cameras, who had built a look I didn't really like in order to make images I didn't really believe in. After years of hard work, how had I wound up in this spot? My box of tricks, my gear, and my ideas about how this should work out were all failing me. At this point, I could have given in. I was tempted to believe that this path was a mistake. Just like a midlife crisis, I toyed with the idea of just buying more gear to compensate, or retreating into denial. I could feel myself flirting with an entitled bitterness toward the world for not giving me what I wanted.

Thankfully, I had learnt about this "two halves" dynamic, so instead, I chose to look for the opportunity to begin moving into the afternoon of my creative journey.

I began to ask myself what was really important to me. Did I really want to be a famous photographer? Was that the goal? When I got really honest, I realised that I didn't care about fame; in fact, I didn't even like the idea when I played it out in my head. In the morning of my journey, I had just assumed that was a good target so I'd run after it, but now it was time to stop and analyse those assumptions. I quickly realised that what I really wanted was to make meaningful work. Whether it was seen by a million people or ten people, I wanted the things I was making to add meaning to their lives and to pull some Order from the Chaos. I couldn't control the number of people who saw my work, but I could start on the long road to building meaning into my making. My priorities had completely shifted, and I now had a new target.

Jung famously said, "We cannot live the afternoon of life according to the program of life's morning, for what was great in the morning will be little at evening, and what in the morning was true, at evening will have become a lie."

It was time to let go of the morning's priorities and step into the afternoon.

&

So what does the "afternoon" look like?

Well, Jung summed it up like this: "The first half of life is devoted to forming a healthy ego, the second half is going inward and letting go of it." He also suggested that in the afternoon we begin to focus more on the things that count, like the people in our lives and the state of the world at large. Our spirituality expands and becomes more inclusive and less rigid. We become less interested in polarizing politics and have a more flexible view of the future. We're more open and less insistent about finding neat or simplistic answers to life. We start to let go of our compulsion for control, and we begin to accept where our influence begins and ends. We start to make friends with uncertainty and paradox.

We also simplify our lives, eliminating all the showy things we've accumulated that were designed to shout about the person we were trying to project into the world. This is certainly done internally but often also physically with our real-world possessions. As we begin to home in on what matters to us and let go of some of our showier assets, we pare down our lives to invest more deliberately in the good stuff we've identified.

As Richard Rohr says, "In the second half we discover that it is no longer sufficient to find meaning in being successful. We need a deeper source of purpose."

Jung called this process "individuation," meaning to "divest the self of false wrappings," which are likely to be the ones we put on in the morning to garner admiration from others. People often misunderstand this phrase because it's obviously rooted in the word "individual" and assume that "individuation" means we have reached our most "separate self," but in fact, the opposite is often true. Those who make it to the afternoon of life—and remember, not everyone does—are the "sages" and the "village elders" in our societies. They are the ones who have cultivated that calm and unthreatened temperament because they let go of their need to impress a long time ago. Now they are able to be there for others in profound ways because their primary drive is no longer limited to their own individual success but has expanded to include the well-being of all. These are most often the individuals who create more meaning in the world for the rest of us.

So what about our creative journeys?

Well, the afternoon is when we similarly put to bed our need to impress and put down our bag of tricks to find out what really matters in our work. We stop obsessing as much about our perceived popularity, and we open up to the idea that our work could really change things for someone. We've realised by now that there are no shortcuts to our goals and even that our objectives may have been the wrong ones to aim for in the first place. Now we might as well get honest about the meaning we want to build into our making so that we can redirect our efforts and begin down the longer road toward a better destination.

For my photography, that meant stripping things back. One of the first things I did when I hit that noon crisis point was to get rid of all the superfluous camera gear I had accumulated. I sold or gave away all my little trick lenses and fancy filters, traded in three backpacks worth of camera equipment, and consolidated down to a basic setup that would fit into one bag. I stopped leaning so heavily on the technical tricks—which had never felt like me anyway. I had adopted them only to impress others and it was time to put the toys away. I returned instead to simple techniques and pushed myself to find more meaningful subject matter to put in front of my lens.

Less gear.

Fewer tricks.

Less attention-seeking.

More substance.

More re-connection.

More meaning.

&

It's important to say that this "two halves" progression is never linear. Most of us will repeat this cycle many times in our lives, in many contexts. I know that when I was reaching the afternoon of my journey with the church, I was only just entering the morning of my journey with photography. Even within photography, I find myself at different stages. My street photography, for example, hasn't yet moved into the afternoon, but I've now learned to enjoy the morning phase and not rush it. When it comes to portrait photography, I've reached high noon, and I'm taking the first baby steps into the afternoon to find more meaning. Any time we start something new, there will always be learning, unlearning, and then relearning to do, and we may find ourselves at very different stages in our different creative pursuits.

That is all good and normal, and the key is not to rush any particular stage because there are things to learn in each, and we need to live both halves fully. If we're still in the morning, then we need to learn to enjoy it and milk it for everything it's worth. There is a real danger if we rush the morning because it may mean that we are ill-prepared for the challenges of the afternoon.

It took me 15 years of working as a photographer to try all those techniques and build that overly fussy style for myself. Only in the last few years have I found the courage to deconstruct the things I'd built and let the metaphorical "box" fall apart after realising the things I'd put inside didn't help me make more meaningful work. The time has now come to reconstruct, but as I've been slowly putting the pieces together, I recognise that nothing that came before was a waste. I will take everything I've learned in the "morning" and the experience of "noon" with me into the "afternoon," where it can only enrich the things I create.

It's also worth saying that reaching the afternoon of our journey doesn't make us any better than anyone else. Our Ego will try and convince us that it makes us "separate and superior," but it's not true. Everyone is at the stage of their journey they should be, and it's possible to make work of great depth and beauty at any stage of development, so concentrate on running your own race and making the very best work you can.

Everything worthwhile takes time. How could it be any other way? I imagine that if you've picked up this book, it's because you've been making things for a while but you want more from your making. This obviously isn't a "quick tips" book so my guess is that it will probably have attracted those of you who are approaching, or moving beyond, your noon, looking for meaning. Building the skills you need to reach competency in your chosen art form has taken a great deal of time in your morning, I'm sure, but the work of the afternoon goes deeper, as you start to ask yourself what you want to point those skills at.

To those of you who have hit your noon crisis point, I hope that you can now see a way forward and won't give up. I know so many artists who throw in the towel at noon. After all, if you've spent this long becoming proficient and your work still feels empty and lacking, it's normal to ask yourself, "What was the point?" For many of us, the next part can be painful as we let our faith in the things we've built crumble, and what comes next will take time to emerge, so we'll need a great deal of patience, not least with ourselves. But if we stick with it and allow ourselves to turn inward and ask the tough questions, we may be able to move into the afternoon of our journey. What feels like a dead end is often a new beginning, a gateway to something more profound if we can only muster the courage to drop the bag of tricks and dig for meaning instead.

It's not a neat process. It isn't the case that my work had no meaning at all five years ago when I was staring out of the office window that Christmas Eve, and today my work is full of meaning. No switch was flipped. Instead, it's been a gradual buildup, which takes substantial time and effort to sustain. However, despite the stops and starts, the progressions and regressions, I can sense myself moving in the right direction overall, and I've learnt to take the pressure off and be kinder to myself.

The work of saturating your making with ever more meaning will take longer than you think. There are no quick wins. It will take setting aside that generative mental space on a regular basis. It requires us to look ourselves squarely in the mirror and get to know ourselves better, and to own our stories. It will mean discovering what we really care about in this world and then working out how to speak about those things with our newfound creative talents. All that's left after that is to set our sights on the distant horizon and take the first of many steps.

As I get older, I've noticed that my perspective is slowly shifting to the longer term. Things like immediate success or recognition for the things I make are now less important to me than legacy. I'm asking myself questions about what I will leave behind when I'm gone, and the potential for these photographs, or films, or books to bring a modicum of meaning to someone else's existential Chaos. Whether that happens today or long after I'm gone is no longer as crucial.

I recently worked with my grandfather on a film, which taught me this lesson. We sat on his sofa while he talked me through the photographs he took during his two years in the Royal Navy, from 1945 to 1947. While in Hong Kong in the aftermath of the Second World War, he had traded a tin of Player's cigarettes for a box Brownie camera, which he then used to take photographs on his tour of duty from Japan to Sri Lanka, Malaysia, China, Australia, and the Mediterranean.

He is 93 years old now, and he's been taking photographs constantly since those early days. He would never consider himself a professional, but his love of the art form is no less passionate for being a "mere" hobbyist. He may not have been trying to create a deliberate "body of work" or have seen himself as an "artist," but he was, and always has been, a "maker of things."

Looking back, there is no way he could have predicted how important those images would be to me, or to history, when he took them. He tells me that at the time he was just taking photographs for his own memories and to show family back home where this young boy from Birmingham had been, and the things he had seen on the other side of the world. But now, with the passage of time, those images hold so much more meaning than he could have predicted.

Some of the stories they tell are horrific, like the images of Japanese prisoners of war, or people trying to rebuild their lives in the ruins of Nagasaki. They describe the Chaos, but they also speak of the relentless human desire to create Order, even in the wake of one of the 20th century's most Chaotic chapters.

Some stories speak of our incredible development as a species, including photographs of Hong Kong, where the tallest buildings were only six stories high, in stark comparison to today's gargantuan forest of skyscrapers. They make me question how fast we're moving and what we might be gaining and losing along the way.

Some of those photographs tell beautiful stories of the very real friendship and affection among young men onboard a Royal Navy frigate, seeing the world for the first time together and missing their loved ones back home.

When I released this little film of my grandfather talking me through his old photo albums, my inbox suddenly filled with emails from people sharing stories about their own grandparents' experiences and showing me their photographs from the war. Think about that: my grandfather made photographs, then decades later I made a film about them, and then in response, people reached out to share their grandparents' own acts of making, in a web of re-connected meaning. Stories upon stories, all because over 75 years ago, my 17-year-old grandfather, while far from home, chose on a whim to pick up a camera and start making images of the world he saw. He didn't achieve any immediate "success" or "fame" from this small but persistent act of making, but the work he produced radiates meaning and rich story. His images are magical artefacts that act as portals to an era and a place shrouded by the mists of time.

I've learnt that the things we make accumulate meaning as they age, not just for others but for ourselves as well. At the close of the film, my grandfather says:

It's wonderful periodically to take my albums out and look back through history. They recall very happy memories, starting with the ship's crew. They were great mates. There was a group of us, all radar operators, who felt the same as I did: "You're never going to see this again." So I took what photographs I could take. It's great. It's something to pass on too. I mean some of my albums start with photographs of my great-grandparents, and here I am sitting at 93 years old in the 21st century looking through them. They're wonderful, and as I've made it very clear to the good Lord, "If I can't take my albums with me, I ain't going!"

If you're making anything at all and you find yourself frustrated that your work isn't appreciated the way you wish it was today, lift up your eyes. Take a longer view of things. There is no way you can predict what the things you make may mean to someone down the road, but I would hazard a guess that if you are faithful to who you are and you uncover your creative voice, if you then persist in your journey to build more and more meaning into your making, the things you create will be incredibly precious to someone someday, just like my grandfather's photo albums are to me.

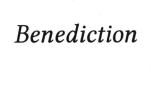

Benediction

If you had found yourself, years ago, sitting and listening to me wrap up a talk in a church, I would have ended with a Benediction of sorts.

In the original Latin, "bene" just means "well," and "diction" comes from the Latin "dicere," which means "say." So, if done right, a "Benediction" isn't just an empty ritual, but rather, a speaker wishing the listeners well after they've spent some time talking about important things.

In some older traditions, a Benediction takes the form of a series of "may you" statements in an effort to make the message personal to you. So, as we close our time together, I'm going to use that simple, ancient formula to send you on your way with some "good words," some "well wishes," and if you'll allow me, maybe even a "blessing."

So, my fellow maker:

May you join with the billions of creative human voices throughout history and attempt to pull Order from Chaos in the small ways you can manage.

May you find ways to tell the capital "T" Truth and to fill your work with Logos.

May you make a habit of taking deep creative in-breaths by carving out generative mental space in order to hear the quiet voices of the Muses.

May you take the challenge to become an autodidact and build a curriculum of creative voices for yourself, which will inflame your imagination.

May you continue to fearlessly face yourself and the journey you've been on and to roll as much of your story into your work as you are willing so that your unique creative voice can emerge.

May you learn to dance well with your Ego and use it to give you the confidence and tenacity to make the things you believe in.

May you let go of your need to control how your work is received and choose instead to focus simply on doing the very best work you can.

May you find the courage to release what you make into the world, where it has the chance to bring comfort and joy to others.

May you find the strength to face your own neediness and drive for approval so that your motivation to make is never tied to the acceptance you receive.

May you learn to recognise the spectre of creative envy when it rears its ugly head, and may you practice generosity with your compliments and free yourself from the imagined competition.

May you learn to tune out the general noise of responses to your work and look instead for feedback from informed and caring commentators.

May you have the modesty to accept compliments with grace, and the humility to learn from even the most pointed criticisms if they come from trusted sources.

May you invest in relationships and find artists you can both learn from and journey with, as you push each other to become the best versions of yourselves.

May you find a mentor you respect who can be your guide, and may you never forget to turn around and offer the same to others.

May you come to trust your feelings and believe that they will lead you toward new avenues of expression, and may you find a balance with your rational mind so that there is stability and consistency in your making.

May you "embrace the shadows"—both those that surface within you and those you pass through—and may you fold them into the things you make in order to present us with a richer, more nuanced view of life.

May you "protect your highlights" and remember to celebrate your growth as an artist and accept yourself as fundamentally good. May your work ultimately point us toward the light.

May you discover your "deep joy" by paying attention to those creative pursuits and subjects that compel you, and use them as compass bearings to explore as you travel onward.

May you find ways to point your "deep joy" at the "world's deep hunger" so as to remake broken connections with the things you create.

May you learn to be patient with yourself and set your sights on the long road ahead, understanding that building anything worthwhile takes time.

May you find ever more meaning in your making.

The Meaning in the Making: The Why and How Behind Our Human Need to Create

Sean Tucker

www.seantucker.photography

Editor: Ted Waitt
Copy editor: Valerie Witte
Project manager: Lisa Brazieal
Marketing coordinator: Mercedes Murray
Interior design, layout, and type: Vladica Stanojevic,
Büro für Visuelle Kommunikation
Cover design: Vladica Stanojevic,
Büro für Visuelle Kommunikation
Cover image: Sean Tucker

ISBN: 978-1-68198-723-1
1st Edition (2nd printing, September 2021)
© 2021 Sean Tucker

Rocky Nook Inc.
1010 B Street, Suite 350
San Rafael, CA 94901
USA

www.rockynook.com

Sean Tucker is a photographer, filmmaker, and author based in the United Kingdom.